ENVIRONMENTAL SECURITY
New Challenges and Role of Military

ENVIRONMENTAL SECURITY
New Challenges and Role of Military

P.K. GAUTAM

Institute for Defence Studies and Analyses, New Delhi

SHIPRA

ISBN: 978-81-7541-524-9

First Published in India in 2010

Environmental Security: New Challenges and Role of Military

Published by:
SHIPRA PUBLICATIONS
H.O.: LG 18-19, Pankaj Central Market, Patparganj,
I.P. Ext., Delhi-110092, Tel: 91-11-22236152, 65277210, 9810522367
Br.Off.115, Munish Plaza, 20, Ansari Road, Darya Ganj,
New Delhi-110002, Tel: 65946453
E-mail: info@shiprapublications.com
www.shiprapublications.com

Preface

In researching the role of the military in environmental security, the three-year fellowship from 2005 to 2008 at the IDSA required the following aspects to be studied:

(a) The state of the environment, ecology and development in our border areas; an analysis of historical degradation, the present state and what the future holds in the next ten to fifteen years as a result of militarisation and preparation for war.
(b) The impact of the changing environment as at (a) above on the planning and conduct of military operations.
(c) The role of the military in a new paradigm of ecological restoration as a step ahead of the existing ETF (ecological task forces).
(d) Military-to-military cooperation with the neighbouring countries to address restoration of watersheds, Himalayan ecology, better sharing of water resources and maritime ecology in an era of confidence-building measures and trust.

Parts of the aspects at (a) and (b) were prepared as papers in the IDSA journal *Strategic Analysis*.[1] This book is about (c) and (d) of the aspects to be studied.

In the first year of my fellowship at the IDSA in early 2006, I was also approached by the Territorial Army Directorate to present a paper on the Vision 2020 Role of Ecological Task Forces (ETF). At the IDSA four papers were presented in Fellows'

1. P.K. Gautam, "Changing Geographic Factors in Planning and Conduct of Indian Military Operations", *Strategic Analysis*, 32(2) (March–April 2008): 245–58; and, "Sino-Indian Water Issues", *Strategic Analysis*, 32(6) (November-December 2008): 969-974.

Seminar in the period and four field visits were made to the eastern, central and western Himalayas and to the Thar Desert. In deciding the areas to be visited, areas where I had not been before were selected provided they related to similar terrain with the neighbouring country. I had already served in Changthang region of Chushul, Siachen glacier and the axis Leh-Zojila astride the Zanskar and Ladakh ranges.

Theoretical insights change after a field visit, supplemented by reading of further literature. After my field trip to Arunachal Pradesh, I read the *Arunachal Pradesh Human Development Report 2005* and the report of the Forest Commission, both seminal contributions to the understanding of ecology and its preservation. My attention was also invited to the work of Sanjib Barua, such as *Post Frontier Blues: Towards a New Policy Framework for Northeast India* (2007), and a special issue on the North-East in the *South Asian Journal*. While my position is that inner line from ecological point of view is a necessary: Barua alludes to the misuse of inner line as it relates to Arunachal Pradesh by locals subletting it to immigrant landless farmers.

In Siang. the bulk of the population believes in Donyi (the Sun) and Polo (the Moon) or Donyi-Poloism, but the population census regarding religion tabulated this religious belief under the column "other", under the rubric of one size fits all. The same mistake can be made when generalising about the North-East. Each region of the North-East is different. Arunachal Pradesh, for example, cannot be studied from any one district. Having spent the first three years of my military career in Kameng in the 1970s I had imagined Siang to be similar, but I found it totally different, with thick Burma or Yunnan type of jungles and low altitude.

In travelling around the Himalayas in my military career I had taken the theory and engineering of road building for granted. It was only after interacting with HQ Border Roads Organisation that I absorbed new insights into the ecological aspects of road building, that while they bring progress they can degrade the ecology, a point that the Forest Commission makes in drawing attention to the need for being sensitive in the matter of road building.

The developments after I visited the Thar Desert also brought new insights. By then the raging conflict in Darfur in Sudan between settled farmers and herders was making news. In the Thar Desert, the advance of canal-based irrigation was marginalising the herders. The Forest Department was fencing the forests for protection and the new gentry of settled agricultural community was fencing off pieces of land called murba. For the herders, common property resources were thus vanishing. Seminal work of J.S. Jodha, such as " Common Property Resources and the Rural Poor", and Kanchan Chopra and S.C. Gulati's work on *Migration, Common Property Resources and Environmental Degradation* (2001) have also shown the struggle of herders.

Four months after my field visit to Rajasthan in summer of 2007, northern India was gripped by the agitation by the Gujars—who are erstwhile nomads—demanding Scheduled Caste (SC) status. Their grievance is about relative deprivation compared with the Scheduled Tribe Minas. The Gujars' demonstrated capacity for political mobilisation was revealing. Compared to the Gujars, herders in Rajasthan such as the Rebaris and Raikas lack a substantial voice and are getting marginalised. In the light of the causes of conflict in Darfur and the Gujar agitation, the emerging socio-economic issues of ecology may have serious internal security implications.

As the population urbanises, new challenges emerge. Urban India with purchasing power is drifting away from matters directly related to biomass, land, livestock and similar mundane but root issues. When I asked the locals employed in the service sector the name of a nearby tree they expressed ignorance. While approaching Jaisalmer I asked the train conductor who is based in the region the name of a beautiful tree with yellow flowers; he did not know. Later, I discovered that the ETF personnel were planting this tree, Rohira, in a big way. A boy at Tattapani in Himachal Pradesh, who had studied at Shimla, could not identify a single tree of his village. Professor Yogendra Alagh remarked that he found no farmer below the age of 60 when he toured Gujarat a few years ago. I saw the same trend in Along in Arunachal Pradesh, at a cattle fair in Magadh region of Bihar, and during a regimental reunion with Sikh friends from the Malwa and Majha regions of Punjab. It could be calamitous if our planning does not allow accommodation for all types and categories of people who depend on land for livelihood.

In studying jhum agriculture I came across two sets of views. The dominant perception is that jhum cultivation is an ecological problem. A contrary point of view argues that jhum demands no fertiliser, no fossil fuel for tractor, and hence in calorie terms it is less energy-intensive. Most of the authors hailing from the jhum-cultivating regions point out that in understanding jhum, one needs to see holistically, to include people's perceptions and customary laws and land tenure system.

This work is a continuation of my research journey. While holding the DRDO D.S. Kothari Chair in 2001-02 at the United Service Institution of India my research was published under the title *Environmental Security: Internal and External Dimensions and Response* (2003). At the IDSA, during the various training capsules, I had to give presentations on environmental matters to Indian Police Service officers, Indian Foreign Service probationers and serving military officers of the intelligence community. These interactive sessions were also used as sounding-boards to get feedback. In my two presentations to class XI students and selected teachers of eco-club of elite public schools in the national capital region in 2007, being conscious that children are not part of the problem of ecological degradation, I had to make them understand that they are part of the solution. These two presentations have been combined as "Teaching global environmental change while overcoming guilt", which is included as Appendix 2 to Chapter 7.

I do not think that there will ever be one agency which can reliably show the extent of degradation of the Himalayas or of other terrains except compartmentalised disciplines. The subject of environment and ecology is dynamic and has many stakeholders. All disciplines claim it as their domain. In the study of environment I am often reminded of Fritjof Capra's quote about Zen in his *Tao of Physics*:

Before you study Zen, mountains are mountains and rivers are rivers; while you are studying Zen, mountains are no longer mountains and rivers are no longer rivers; but once you have enlightenment, mountains are once again mountains and rivers again rivers.

Acknowledgements

Had it not been for the motivation for fieldwork I would never have learnt and known what I now understand about the ETF (ecological task forces). For this I thank the Director General IDSA, Shri N.S. Sisodia, who has emphasised the value of fieldwork by researchers. I also need to thank Shri Virendra Gupta, IFS, JS and Deputy Director IDSA who approved my field trip programme, based on which I got the budgetary support and sanction to carry out my visit, and our Accounts Officer Shri Ramesh K. Aurora and his team for helping me navigate the route of financial bills with precision. The photographs of my field visit to the Thar Desert, Arunachal Pradesh and Himachal Pradesh were published in the new-look Annual Report 2006-07 of the IDSA, for which I thank Dr Thomas Mathew, IAS, JS and Deputy Director General and his editorial team of Kalyan, Krishnappa and Arpita Anant.

I would like to thank Maj Gen P. Rajagopal, AVSM, VSM, ADG (TA) for inviting me to present a paper in the Vision 2020 seminar of the Territorial Army in 2006, which led me to work on the theoretical framework of my project, and for later granting permission for the field visit to three locations where the ETF of the TA are deployed. Lt Col Dhall of TA-2 was very helpful in timely communication of my visit programme. Lt Gen Rao, DG BRO was kind enough to allow me to interact with his staff at Delhi on ecological aspects of road building. Col Prakash Tewari, Director (Policy) Ecology was kind in inviting my attention to the Green Governance pages of the Bombay Natural History Society and in sharing ideas. I am also thankful to his successor, Col Anuj Singh Sidhu, for keeping me in the picture on the major aspects of ecological thinking.

Rajasthan

Col Shardul Singh (Retd), the first Officer Commanding, was kind in giving his oral historical version of ETF in Rajasthan in the 1980s. Thanks to Lt Col P.S. Rathore, the CO of 128 ETF and his fine team for providing me accommodation and showing me around the entire battalion area over two days and evenings by road and on foot. The men hailing from Rajputana displayed an intense devotion to the tough ecological restoration. This gave me an insight about how important it is to have regional troops under regional regiments from the ecological point of view. I thank the staff of the Central Arid Zone Research Institute (CAZRI) at Jaisalmer for showing me their medicinal plant nursery. Director General CAZRI Jodhpur and his team were very helpful in sending copies of their research on the Thar Desert and inviting my attention to their open access and excellent work on strategies to counter desertification. Thanks to the staff of the Agricultural Department extension farm of the Government of Rajasthan for explaining the work in progress and allowing me to taste the delicious hybrid ber developed by them, besides showing me the crop of zeera which had been destroyed by unseasonal rain. They also enlightened me that now the largest mandi of gram (channa) is in Hanumangarh in north Rajasthan—thanks to the irrigation water of the east-flowing rivers. Monalisa Joshi, who hails from Jodhpur gave valuable comments on an earlier draft of the chapter.

Kumaon

I thank Captain Amit of 130 Infantry Battalion (TA) Ecological and his dedicated team of Junior Commissioned Officers and senior Non-Commissioned Officers. They deserve special thanks for showing me the old sites as well as those of the current year and also sharing with me their traditional ecological knowledge over three days and treating me as their regimental officer. Medha Bist, who hails from Kumaon and also had worked in the rural interior regions before joining

IDSA, gave valuable comments on an earlier draft of the chapter and also shared literature on forestry of the region for which I am thankful.

Himachal Pradesh and Punjab

I thank Brig J.S. Thind, Deputy Director General, Territorial Army, HQ Western Command and staff for the administrative help. I acknowledge the excellent briefing done by Lt Col K.L. Petkar, CO 133 ETF, and Major Deepak Kumar the Adjutant at Kufri and Major Sarban Singh the company commander for showing me the plantation area and the terrain at Tattapani.

For the second phase of my visit to the Sutlej watershed till near the Sino-Indian border I am gratful to Maj Gen P.C. Kharbanda, Major General (General Staff) HQ Western Command for granting me permission and providing administrative support and also reception and area familiarisation by elements of the Indian Army serving at Pooh and beyond. Special thanks to the Brigade Major (now called Brigade GSO1) Lt Col Jangid and all ranks of 13 Grenadiers. Lt Col Ajai Vashisht at Rampur gave me some idea of hydroelectric projects such as the one at Nathpa Jhakri. Col Virendra Sahai Verma (Retd), a scholar of Buddhism as practised in the Himalayas, was kind enough to give me contact details of Shri D.S. Negi, IAS of Pooh. I could not meet Shri Negi, but his wife gave me valuable insights into ecological matters of the Pooh region of Kinnaur. It was not the first time I realised how diverse India is: Negi is not necessarily a Hindu name; Negis, I learnt, may be Buddhists as well. I also need to compliment Shri Karmjit Singh and later his replacement Shri Sangat Singh, the civilian driver of the taxi for having driven so well in rough terrain.

Later in September I travelled to Faridkot for regimental reunion and there saw the Hussainiwala headworks on the India–Pakistan border, for which I thank Col R.S. Athreye for his help. Although the Indus Water Treaty permits zero flow into Pakistan, the Sutlej flows in parts, even majestically into Pakistan. It is impossible to divert all flows and one cannot divide nature. On my journey from Faridkot till Pathankot I was accompanied by former Havildar and war veteran colleague and now retired Subedar Major Darshan Singh, who gave me a run-down of agricultural practices in Malwa and Manjha regions of Punjab. Besides confirming that the youth are now least interested in agriculture which is mostly mechanised, he also informed me that due to cost-benefit analysis of transport, paddy husk is burnt and only wheat residue is collected as fodder. For my travels along the Beas watershed from Pathankot till Dharamsala I thank Brigadiers S.S. Sangra and A.K. Misra who also facilitated my stay at Yol Camp.

Arunachal Pradesh, Assam, Meghalaya and Other Regions of North-East India

Thanks to Brig Tony Bardolai, my former colleague at the USI, who while commanding a brigade in the Lohit Region gave a practical framework to my visit to Siang. What I had envisaged from a look at the map would take a day took two days. Thanks to Brigadier Bardolai I had a workable plan which made me derive the maximum benefit. He insisted that the real Brahmaputra was the Lohit and I need to visit that sector to get a real feel of the Brahmaputra. Formations and units of 4 Corps provided magnanimous support, prompted by Lt Gen Deepak Kapoor, AVSM, SM, VSM, ADC Vice Chief of the Army Staff and his secretariat. The support, facilitation and encouragement of Lt. Gen. R.K. Chhabra, AVSM, VSM, GOC 4 Corps, the Chief of Staff Maj Gen S.C. Sharma, VSM in particular, Maj Gen N.C. Marwah, GOC 2 Mountain Division, Brig M.M.S. Rai, Commander 5 Mountain Brigade, CO and all ranks of the 9th Battalion the Kumaon Regiment, military ferry of 236 Inland Water Transport Operating Unit Engineers, E Company 20 Battalion ITBP and keeper of IB at Gelling Shri Dorji Sangal are hereby recorded with gratitude. Many thanks to 44 Border Road Task Force/105 Road Construction Company of the Border Roads Organisation and its Regimental Medical Officer and staff for accommodation and insights into the local conditions and to transit camp Likabali for entry and exit to the region from the foothills.

I also thank Shri Mukteja Rehman of Dibrugarh, the driver of the so-called CHT in military parlance (civil hired transport), which was a Bolero for my trip from the foothills of Arunachal Pradesh to the international border, and ex-Subedar D.K. Sethia, the owner-cum-driver of the second Bolero for my return journey through Assam, for sharing insights and their experience, and driving their vehicles deftly and safely. I specially thank Quarter Master General Branch and Staff of HQs 2 Mountain Division and 5 Mountain Brigade for timely hiring of civil transport, including budgeting for it from their side.

I thank Professor K.K. Barua, faculty members, research staff and students of the Department of Environmental Science, Tezpur University, for organising interaction and demonstrating fieldwork and lab analysis for measuring methane from paddy field. I learnt much from Professor Barua when we interacted for three days during the seminar in September 2006. Other academics from universities in the region who shared ecological insights are Lt Gen S.K. Pillai, PVSM (Retd) and Professors Joykumar Singh and Ibo Singh from Manipur University, Imphal. Thanks to Ashild Kolas from the Peace Research Institute, Oslo, who while visiting IDSA in 2007 discussed jhum with me and shared her understanding of it from hill-valley dynamic in the North-East using the World System theory of Immanuel Wallerstein. In her view, jhum has been given a bad name. She found my USI research on jhum and other ecological roots of insurgency very informative.

I visited Meghalaya in March and September 2006 when the IDSA asked me to organise a seminar jointly with the North East Council and North East Hill University. Visiting the place after the 1971 war experience I witnessed an example of the rapid and unplanned urbanisation and forest degradation taking place in the hill stations all over India, including massive traffic jams on the hill roads. My meetings with people and discussions on ecological issues helped me to shape my chapter on the broad ecological issues of the North-East. I specially thank Mr Peter Thorose, Principal, St Peter's College, Shillong for sparing his time and sharing his experiences. He showed me a video movie which he had shot on poaching in Assam and how with the help of an unarmed ecological team of civilians he was unable to stop this. Thanks to Ms Sujata Kanungo for insights concerning Shillong and its neighbourhood.

I benefited from insights of Manipuris at IDSA such as N. Neihsial, Amarjeet Singh, and Thangjam Khruschev Singh; Assamese hill dweller from Haflong Namrata Goswami; Pushpita Das, a Bengali born and brought up in Arunachal Pradesh; and Col Gurinder Singh, a Sikh to all appearances but a Naga at heart. Sreeradha Dutta, an expert on the security and ethnicity of the region, also gave valuable insights. The seminar in Shillong also had the local media. They interviewed all participants from IDSA and the programme was telecast in the region.

I thank Dr M.V. Rappai for inviting me to give a presentation at the Institute of Chinese Studies in March 2008 on the ecological issues of Arunachal Pradesh based on my field trip. My attention was invited by Patricia Oberoi of the institute to works such as Sanjib Barua's *Post Frontier Blues: Towards a New Policy Framework for Northeast India* (2007) and a special issue on the North-East in the *South Asian Journal*. Such writings are rare and welcome and I benefited from reading them.

Cluster Members and Other Professors

Special thanks to my cluster members Shebonti Ray Dadwal, Uttam Sinha, J. Nandakumar and Priyadarshini Singh. My former guide Professor Subhash Chander was always willing to answer my queries on water-related issues. He also came as a discussant for one of my Fellows Seminars about sharing of water resources with China. I will value his scientific and practical insights. I thank Professor C.K. Varshney for his encouragement during my Fellows Seminar in 2006 and also for chairing a brainstorming session held at the IDSA on environmental matters.

Delhi

The first ETF I visited was 132 ETF restoring the Bhatti mines in the erstwhile Tughlaqabad field firing ranges in November 2005. My second vist was in January 2009. I thank Colonels Pareek, and Semwal, and Majors Ahlawat and Pratul Thapliyal and their dedicated team led by Subedar Major Amar Singh in explaining the restoration work done including how they achieved a CDM project.

I am thankful to Professor C.R. Babu and Dr Amit Love for my visit to the Centre for Environmental Management of Degraded Ecosystem, School of Environmental Studies, University of Delhi, in August and November 2005.

I am also thankful to Dr Kishan Kumar and Dr Anil Singh of the Central Road Research Institute for their help. Dr Anil Kumar needs a special mention as he suggested that I meet one such pioneer of the topic, Dr A.P. Mitra, with whom he had worked in working out the First National Communication (Natcom) of India. I interviewed Dr A.P. Mitra in December 2005 and learnt a great deal about climate change and the new challenges of environmental protection. His humility was infectious. Later I wrote an obituary on him in *Current Science* (15 November 2007). I also thank the staff of the Central Soil and Material Research Station, New Delhi. Thanks to Dr Kishore Kumar of the Society for Indian Ocean Studies for inviting me to attend all their environment-related events. Special thanks to Ms Nita Ganguli of Sanskriti School and Ms Shalini Datta of Summerfield School for inviting me to interact with schoolchildren.

Library and Other Staff

I thank the library staff of the IDSA, United Service Institution of India and The Energy Research Institute for their support. Raj Kumar Tripathi and Mukesh Dabas were most helpful in keeping my internet, computer, printer and ink supply in good order.

Contents

1

Introduction

War, Preparation for War and Ecology

With improvements in the destructive potential of weapons or as denial of resources in wartime tactics, substantial and long-term ecological damage is caused by warfare. The destruction of ecology by the use of nuclear weapons in World War II and scorched-earth policy in war histories have been well recorded. The use of defoliation agents by the US military in Vietnam, the destruction of the marshes in Iraq and the burning of oil wells by the retreating Iraqi troops in the First Gulf War are landmark events on the subject.

Ironically, most of our border areas, which are highly militarised, are also ecologically fragile regions. The first war after independence was in Jammu and Kashmir in the fragile Himalayan region as were all later conflicts with Pakistan and China. The Siachen glacier has been militarised for over two decades. The preparation for war also takes a toll of ecology. Massive deforestation has taken place in the Himalayas for preparing and maintaining defences from logs or to clear the field of fire or in road building. Combined with the massive conventional preparation many insurgencies since independence have taken their toll of ecology. Deforestation and environmental degradation is invariably the outcome.

Road construction and maintenance has its peculiar sets of problems. The Himalayan terrain is highly seismic with active tectonic belts. It is unstable and is liable to flooding, slides (rock, soil, mud or combination), snowdrifts, frost, avalanches, glacier activity, aggrading of riverbeds, etc., which affect road construction and maintenance. Himalayas are the youngest mountain system in the world. A senior geologist has known to have remarked in a lighter vein, "You have commenced road construction a bit too early in the Himalayas, maybe a few million years ahead".[1]

The Stockholm International Peace Research Institute (SIPRI) in its yearbook highlights the fact each year cogently that the incidence of interstate wars is declining. Nevertheless, owing to realist reasons military preparation and troop deployment is the norm in the Himalayas by India against Pakistan and China. Beginning 2007/08, nearly five decades after having fought a border war, India and China are conducting joint military exercises. This may be the right time for the two countries to exchange ideas, notes and good practices of ecological restoration in the fragile Himalayas.

Many changes have taken place in the ecology and environment in our other border regions as well. Multi-cropping in the plains of Punjab and north Rajasthan is the norm. The canal network is spreading with unregulated use of ground water. The linking of rivers may provide more obstacles and areas prone to waterlogging and thus deny approaches or become obstacles. Urbanisation, industrialisation and demographic growth have changed the ecology in our border regions.

Thus it is not that the military is repairing damages done as due to war. Rather the repairs that are being undertaken are the damage to the ecology due to unsustainable use of natural resources. There is also no classical enemy. We ourselves our are own enemies. Now this is nothing new. Ecology is a war against ourselves. It is war where mainstream economic theories clash with ecological principles. One common way scholars express this is that if economic growth is the accelerator, ecology is the break.

The suggested involvement of the military in ecological conservation is primarily on account of military discipline. Planting a tree may be a great event for the media cameras, but what is important is survival of the planted trees. Even preparing to plant a tree requires a number of labour-intensive skills. The pit has to be dug. If it is on a hill slope, one has to climb. Water and manure have to be arranged. Saplings suitable to the micro-climate have to be nurtured in a nursery. A plan has to be made well before the monsoon. The planted saplings have to be protected, requiring sustained and systematic work by a motivated and disciplined set-up. Bursts of inspiration or spurts of vision cannot deliver this type of work. The military, with its inherent regimental system and having troops from the rural background has an added advantage to undertake this task. Most of the soldiers retire after colour service in their mid-thirties. The pension they receive needs to be supplemented with additional income. Unlike in the past, most of the troops do own agricultural land. It is in this context that ETF assumes importance. On whether it means militarisation of the environment and the military building up its so-called empire, the foresters probably are divided in their views.

The other Services of the armed forces also play a part in ecological conservation. Part of the charter of the Coast Guard, for example, is preservation and protection of the marine environment and prevention and control of marine pollution. The coastal region is under massive threat of land-based pollution from effluent or agricultural runoff or discharge of untreated liquid waste from built-up areas. Sea-based pollution occurs on account of oil spills from oil tankers and maritime pollution disasters.

While the destruction of ecology is inherent in war or its preparation, the military is also a potent force for ecological restoration. All the three Services are role models in ecological services. The automatic greening of all military stations in the country bears this out. This greening ethos of the military is a great national asset. The forces also have an opportunity to serve in all the fragile border regions and are thus the best "sensors" of ecological health from the ground, coastal areas, oceans and the air.

The Ecological Task Forces (ETF) are unique to India. The contribution of the ETFs of the Territorial Army has been well recognised over decades. Scholars have urged expansion of their role to revitalising of wetlands, stalling desertification, help in overcoming waterlogging and salinisation, and so on. The armed forces in integration with the states concerned can provide the organisation, ethos and leadership. Ecological restoration provides an opportunity for employment by way of organisation of the workforce on the lines of the ETF. Some studies show that maximum employment generation is in this particular area of ecological restoration.

Field Visits

For this study the following field visits were made. (a) *Ecological Task Forces*: one ETF each in the Thar Desert (being closest to Pakistan), Pithoragarh district of Kumaon Himalaya in Uttarakhand (being closest to Nepal) and in the Sutlej watershed at Tattapani in Himachal Pradesh. (b) *Sutlej, Beas and Ravi Watersheds* (2007): the Sutlej watershed till Pooh in Kinnaur district was visited along the river, including Nathpa Jhakri where massive hydroelectric works are being undertaken; the Hussainiwala headwork where the Sutlej enters Pakistan; the confluence of Beas and Sutlej at Harike headworks; the Beas watershed from Pathankot to Dharamshal in western Himachal Paradesh and the Pong dam on the Beas; Madhopur headworks on the Ravi watershed; Thein or Ranjit Sagar Dam. (c) *The North-East*: two visits were undertaken to study the Meghalayas in and around Shillong in March and September 2006 in connection with a seminar held in Shillong on the topic "Peace and Development in the North East", which had as its focus the ecological threats to the North-East. A field visit to the Department of Environmental Science at Tezpur University in April 2007 helped in writing on the unique issues concerned with climate change. (d) Field visits were also made to Arunachal Pradesh to study the watershed on the Siang (Dihang) which in Tibet is known as Yarlung Tsangpo. The northern plains of Brahmaputra valley were also visited.

Scheme of Chapters

Theoretical knowledge combined with experience while

serving in the various regions, a continuous study of environmental literature, effort to come to an understanding of environment security by way of participation in various debates, and fieldwork specific to study ecology has helped shape this book. From a scholarly perspective, the environment is the dependent variable and human activity is the independent variable, while climate change is the intervening variable. There is no ready and proven theory of environmental degradation to be tested. Poverty is not the greatest polluter; the rich and industrial world consumes more material and energy in production and sustains the trend in consumption and generates more solid, liquid and gaseous waste. The aim of this work has been to study and assess the activities being undertaken by the military in ecological conservation. In doing so, fresh insights may be available on issues not only of environment but also how people relate their lives to nature in a rapidly industrialising India. In the light of the findings of this research policy measures on some environmental issues have also been suggested.

NOTES

1. D.S.N. Ayyar, *History of the Border Roads Organisation, Volume I, Organisation and History 1960–1995*, New Delhi: Directorate General Border Roads, 1996, p. 27.

2

Ecological Task Force (ETF) and Ecological Institutions of the Indian Army

An Overview

Introduction

The Indian Army is probably the only army in the world which has implemented the concept of ecological units of the Territorial Army since the 1980s. These units, called Ecological Task Forces (ETF), are officered by a mix of regular and Territorial Army officers and based on the manpower of young ex-servicemen. ETFs are funded by the state government and the Ministry of Environment and Forests. The ETFs through tree plantation have performed admirably in recvoering from the damage of manmade ecological disasters such as the mined areas in the Mussoorie hills or sand dune stabilisation in the Thar desert of Rajasthan and other places in the Himalayas and the foothills. Over the last decade the ETFs have planted approximately two crore plants and have reclaimed twenty-five mines.[1]

The credit for the ETF concept goes to Dr Norman Borlaugh, the father of the Green Revolution, who in the early 1980s suggested the need for a disciplined force to undertake such tasks. Prime Minister Indira Gandhi, on observing the ecological degradation in the Himalayas, displayed a rare ecological insight and operationalised the idea by an executive decision to form ETF of the Territorial Army. New-age soldier scholars, including Brigadier Michael Harbottle of the United Kingdom (UK) were inspired by the ETF. Brigadier Harbottle recorded the unique work of the ETF in his path-breaking work, *What is Proper Soldiering*,[2] which seems to have set off the trend of employing the armed forces all over the world. They are just not fighting each other, but are being used in disaster relief, ecological restoration and UN peacekeeping missions, which demands deep understanding of ecological links to intra-state wars and ultimate peace. The link of ecological restoration and peace got better recognition when in 2004 Wangari Maathai, Kenya's Assistant Minister of Environment, Natural Resources and Wildlife was awarded the Nobel Peace Prize for planting trees.

ETF in Brief

There are currently eight ETFs (*see* Table 2.1). An ETF has the headquarter-cum-administrative element and a company under an officer, three Junior Commissioned Officers (JCOs) and about 99 men. The strength of an ETF consisting of HQ and one company may be three officers, five JCOs and 139 other ranks, making a total of 147 all ranks; a two-company ETF would be nearly 250 all ranks. Local assistance from the Forest Department is taken in imparting training. One advantage with the massive rural base of our soldiers is that they have a very good working knowledge of agriculture, forestry and tasks close to Mother Nature. But soon this inherent advantage will reduce due to urbanisation.

The initiative to raise an ETF is taken by the state which needs to solve an ecological problem in a timeframe of say three to five years. Generally, the budget is shared by the state government and the Union Ministry of Environment and Forests (MoEF). The ETFs of the Union Territory of Delhi and Himachal Pradesh are fully financed by the state government, whereas the two new raisings in Assam are financed fully by the MoEF. This joint venture of the MoEF, Ministry of Defence and state government concerned undertakes activities such as afforestation, soil and water conservation, pasture development and other restorative works As a thumb rule, the capability of

Table 2.1. ETFs as in 2008

ETF (Regimental Affiliation)	*State/Year of Raising*	*Tasks*	*Remarks*
127 Infantry Battalion (TA) Ecological (Garhwal Rifles)	Uttarakhand/1982	(a) Has completed soil conversation in area Mohand of Siwalik ranges (b) Restoration of Agar watershed north of Mussoorie hills in progress	Two-company ETF till 2008; two additional companies sanctioned in April 2008 on the initiative of the Government of Uttarakhand
128 Infantry Battalion (TA) Ecological (Rajputana Rifles)	Rajasthan/1983	(a) Completed afforestation in area Pugal till Indira Gandhi Canal and creation of Amarpura lake (b) Converting Mohangarh in Jaiselmer district into green fields	Two company ETF
129 Infantry Battalion (TA) Ecological (Jammu and Kashmir Light Infantry)	Jammu and Kashmir/1988	(a) Restored catchments and watershed in at Samba (Kandi in the local language) (b) Afforestation and soil conservation in progress in Bahu Jindra mountain range	One company with affiliated forest department personnel
130 Infantry Battalion (TA) Ecological (Kumaon Regiment)	Uttarakhand/1994	(a) Restoration of forest wealth in Kumaon region in area Pithoragarh	Two-company ETF; two additional companies sanctioned in April 2008 on the initiative of the Government of Uttarakhand
132 Infantry Battalion (TA) Ecological (Rajput Regiment)	Union Territory of Delhi/First company in 2000 and second company in 2005	(a) Converting barren and mined land of Bhatti mines to a thick forest and park (b) Compensatory plantation in area Ujawa near Najafgarh	(a) Two-company ETF financed by the Delhi gov. (b) In early 2009, the only ETF to have claimed carbon credit through clean development mechanism under the Kyoto Protocol through sponsorship by Germany.
133 Infantry Battalion (TA) Ecological (Dogra Regiment)	Himachal Pradesh/2006	Ecological restoration of Sutlej basin	One-company ETF
134 and 135 Infantry Battalions (TA) Ecological (Assam Regiment)	Assam (Rangia and Tamalpur respectively)/2007	Afforestation	(a) Both units are three-company ETFs funded by the Ministry of Environment and Forests (b) Raising budget is Rs 16 crore

Source: Additional Directorate Territorial Army, *The Citizen's Army*, New Delhi: Lancer, 2005; updates by the author.

an ETF is to plant 1.5 lakh saplings a year in 200 acres of land in the hills and 400 acres in the plains. Empirical data show a very high survival rate of the plants (varying from 70 to 87%).[3] The rough cost of an ETF embodied for eight months in a year is Rs 1.83 crore for five years.[4]

The ETF is raised and embodied for the task. On completion of the task in three to five years the unit hands over the eco-regenerated area to the state government, after which it may be disbanded. Till date, all the four ETFs raised in the 1980s and 1990s have been redeployed. Uttarakhand has two ETFs of four companies each.

The following requirements have to be met to form an ETF.

- (a) A problem of environmental degradation demanding military type discipline and dedication. This should be known to the leaders at both the centre and in the state.
- (b) Political will, including allocation of budget.
- (c) Sizeable ex-servicemen population needs to be residing in the region.
- (d) There needs to be a well-oiled civil-military interface for smooth implementation of the scheme.
- (e) Regular officers should be available to be posted by the Military Secretary's Branch of Army Headquarters, failing which TA offices intake can be beefed up as a long-term strategy.[5]

The Armed Forces

Though non-mandated, all the three Services inherit an ethos of environmental awareness. This at first blush appears strange. The military, after all, is the main instrument of destroying the environment with its military might and firepower. But as the saying goes, soldiers who have seen war are the best ambassadors of peace. Similarly, military life and routine in both field and peace areas stresses the need for environmental awareness and preservation. The high order of natural capital in the military garrisons is witness to this phenomenon. Each unit and station has an arboriculture plan.

The Indian Army has an ecological cell at the Army HQ. It is routine for a formation such as a Division to organise events related to ecology and environment.

Because of the nature of military deployment military personnel are posted and deployed in ecologically sensitive and rugged terrain such as deserts, jungles, mountains and island territories. With frequent postings and transfers in their military career, the personnel get to know the biodiversity of the nation. They also carry with them traditional ecological knowledge and wherever posted apply the best practices like tree plantation and nurturing. This love for nature is also a function of the need for soldiers to have an eye for the ground. They also train for war in jungles, mountains, riverine and desert terrain. Military life thus is a free on-the-job package on ecology.

Great care is exercised in avoiding damage to land during training and manoeuvres. Compensation is paid to locals for any damage done. Most field firing ranges are acquired. Due to urbanisation and the need for land, there has been a steady decrease in notified areas. The military has adjusted to this new challenge by switching over to simulators. However, there is a limit to simulation and imagination when it comes to training in soldierly skills and large-scale exercises. A standing military needs to train. There is thus at places a clash of interest of the damage done due to exercises versus not carrying out any training. It is unlikely that this will ever get resolved.

One also has to be careful in expecting the military to ignore its core competency of soldiering, combat and war fighting. Long periods of peace may induce a misguided opinion to use the military for tasks other than their primary mission. A military is worth only if it is prepared for war. Any digression will pose serious challenges to national security. What in fact the military leadership needs to know is the ecological roots of conflict and environmental factors as a cause of war. In the nuclear context, Bernard Brodie noted that "Thus far the chief purpose of our military establishment has been to win wars. From now on its chief purpose must be to avert them. It can have almost no other useful purpose." In similar manner, the military needs to be aware of the causes of war and help the nation take all measures to avoid war due to ecological degradation.

NOTES

1. Additional Directorate Territorial Army, *The Citizen's Army*, New Delhi: Lancer, 2005, p. 41.
2. Brigadier Michael Harbottle, *What is Proper Soldiering*. For a book review see *British Army Review*, No. 103, April 1993.
3. *The Citizen's Army*, n. 1, pp. 94–105.
4. Presentation made by Brig. G.S. Dhillon, SM, TA Group Commander, Western Command during the TA seminar Vision 2020 in February 2006.
5. *The Citizen's Army*, n. 1. The ETF can perform well with Junior Commissiosned Officers also as there is a chronic shortage of young officers. Raising of new ETFs should not get stalled in future on the pretext of shortage of officers.

3

The Desert Region

Introduction

The 32.7 million hectares (mha) of hot arid region of India is spread over Rajasthan (61.9%), Gujarat (19.6%), Haryana and Punjab (8.65%), Andhra Pradesh (6.8%), Karnataka (2.7%) and Maharashtra (0.4%). Low and erratic rainfall, extreme temperatures, strong wind velocity, low humidity and frequent droughts characterise its ecosystem.[1] Wind erosion accounts for 13.00 mha land in India, of which 10.75 mha (82.69%) is in western Rajasthan. The ecology of the Thar desert of Rajasthan is very fragile. This densely populated desert is under additional pressures of ecological degradation due to population pressures, economic growth, changing livelihood patterns and urbanisation. The transfer of water of the eastern rivers of the Indus has been a landmark event in slowly turning the command area green and stabilisation of sand dunes or even flattening of areas of sand dunes for agriculture. Irrigation without proper drainage brings in the perennial problems of salinity and waterlogging besides changing the ecology. This chapter is based on a field visit to an Army unit undertaking sand dune stabilisation in the canal command.

Just focusing on the narrow input-output job of an ETF is not enough. Many interactions at the human social level also take place as the task force performs its job. This chapter attempts to relate the ecological work with the larger picture of change in the lifestyle of the rural people and ecology. It shows how focusing on just one driver of economic growth (like grain production and converting desert into agricultural plots) will create unintended problems elsewhere.

Three issues are central to the study of the Thar desert, namely, the threat of desertification and its spread, greening of the desert by transfer of river waters and ecological challenges associated with it, and the human interface or how greening of the region affects pastoralists and also the change from subsistence to commercial farming.

Desertification

Post-independence planners were worried about the threat of drylands and desertification. In view of the seriousness of the problem the UN had even declared the year 2006 as the International Year for Deserts and Desertification. Studies by the United Nations Environmental Programme (UNEP) have shown that the problem of land degradation is worsening. In the past, drylands recovered easily following long droughts and dry periods. However, under modern conditions they tend to lose their biological and economic productivity quickly unless they are managed in a sustainable manner.[2] The international community has long recognised that desertification is a major economic, social and environmental problem of concern to many countries in all regions of the world. The Convention to Combat Desertification (CCD) entered into force in 1996. Though the CCD is primarily focused on Africa, its central ecological underpinning is relevant to our study. It defines and elaborates:

(a) "desertification" means land degradation in arid, semi-arid and dry sub-humid areas resulting from various factors, including climatic variations and human activities;

(b) "combating desertification" includes activities which are part of the integrated development of land in arid, semi-arid and dry sub-humid areas for sustainable development which are aimed at:

   (i) prevention and/or reduction of land degradation;
   (ii) rehabilitation of partly degraded land; and
   (iii) reclamation of desertified land.[3]

Greening

Rajasthan is being greened by the transfer of water of the three eastern rivers of the Indus basin, namely, Beas, Sutlej and Ravi. While negotiating for the Indus Water Treaty with Pakistan in the 1950s, the Indian argument to green the desert for food security and rising populations was instrumental in getting our share of the eastern rivers. The Rajasthan Main Canal, now called Indira Gandhi Neher Prayojna (IGNP), is a result of this historical process. Transfer of water to an arid region has its set of problems of wind erosion which shifts sand and chokes the canals. Another problem is waterlogging and salinity and the advent of settled agriculture in an earlier dryland and scanty rain-fed farming. The entire Indus basin, including Punjab and parts of Pakistan, is facing this twin problem. Wind erosion particularly affects the arid zones of Jaisalmer. With the advent of IGNP, massive shelter-belt plantation work was undertaken to check silting of canal through wind-blown sand.[4] The Indian Army and Green Governance project through the Bombay Natural History Society had organised workshops in 2004 at the desert-based 12 Corps on the theme of Water Conservation and Ground Water Rejuvenation, and Protection and Conservation of endangered Wildlife of Thar Desert.[5]

Pastoralists

Greening has transformed large areas from subsistence and rain-fed farming to commercial farming, displacing graziers to non-command areas, thus exerting even more pressure on the already overgrazed countryside.[6] At times, this displacement has led to violent conflict. One may recall that in conflict-torn Darfur in Sudan Arab nomadic herders had lived amicably with black settled farmers who welcomed herders as they criss-crossed the land, grazing their camels and sharing wells. But once the rain stopped, the farmers fenced their land for fear it would be ruined by the passing herds. With not enough food and water, fighting broke out.[7] In India the problem is shrinking of grasslands and common property resources for grazing. We shall revert to this topic after having a look at the efforts being made by the ETF.

Visit to 128 Infantry Battalion (TA) Ecological

128 Infantry Battalion, Territorial Army (Ecological) Rajputana Rifles was initially raised and deployed for desert stabilisation campaign on the left bank of the Indira Gandhi (IG) main canal in Amarpura area (approximately 100 km from Bikaner). The unit, which is a three-company model (total strength 4 officers, 13 Junior Commissioned Officers and 530 Other Ranks), accomplished the challenging task of afforestation of the area from 1983 to 1996.[8] Over 1.1 crore (101 million) saplings were planted on 7330 hectares, as also grass slips for pasture development over 3540 hectares on the west bank of IG main along the Bajju-Pugal road in Bikaner district.[9] Having accomplished this challenging task, the unit moved to Mohangarh where it commenced work in May 1997, amidst temperatures ranging from 49 degrees C during the summer to sub-zero during the winter. The main task is to carry out sand dune stabilisation in areas around Mohangarh/Nachna and to create shelter and green belt around IG canal. From 1997 till end of 2006 it has planted over 18.25 lakh saplings in about 2668 hectares of forest land. The effect of the tremendous greening effort is best seen on the 60 km stretch of land on the right side of the Bajju-Pugal road on the west bank of IG canal.

The fieldwork and visit was from 20 to 22 February 2007 in area Mohangarh. The ETF is charged with afforestation of Forest Department land adjacent to the tail end of the IGNP. Each of its three companies (an average of one officer, 3 JCOs and 150 Other Ranks) deploys in a given area theoretically for three years. It is expected that in three years the saplings take root and do not need sustained year-round protection. It is no more a military-like task and the area is handed over to the civil administration.

For the financial year 2006-7 the Forest Department allotted 580 hectares. Each hectare is planted with 800 saplings. For planting in 100 hectares 150 troops are required. Catering for 20 per cent replacement, the total saplings planted are 4,60,000. In forestry the survival rate is the measure of success. The present survival rate is 90 to 95 per cent. Planting takes place in July-August, when monsoon rains are expected. Before that preparation of pits and allied activities is undertaken, which includes provisioning and setting up of improvised water storage structures, preparation of saplings in unit nursery, taking over plants from forest nursery, and so on. Thus at any one time the troops of a company ETF are distributed over three working areas and the battalion would have nine such blocks of about 2000 hectares under its charge spread out over an area of 50 to 60 km radius. Sparse deployment can lead to problems of command, control, communications and logistics. These problems are overcome using the military methods of maintaining troops as in any defence. This unique terrain and situation is best overcome by the military ethos of an ETF with the commitment of all ranks.

The Commanding Officer Lt Col P.S. Rathore accompanied by Capt Vinay Sharma and Sub Maj G.S. Tanwar showed the entire area by road and on foot. More than 200 km was covered in two days. All areas of present plantation, future plantations commencing April 2007 and handed-over plantations were shown in great detail, including the amazing improvisation to water and protect the plants. The Forest Department nursery and Rajasthan State Agricultural Research Station in the area was also visited, where the officials gave a briefing on the work in progress. It was heartening to see the intense devotion to the tough work by all ranks.[10] Great pains were taken for imparting a working knowledge to a visitor like me to understand and identify ecologically suitable plants and shrubs such as Acacia Tortilis, Khejri, Angrezi babool, Desi babool, Rohira, sewan grass, ber, and so on. Appendix 2 lists some types of plants.

Afforestation and allied work in this harsh terrain is not an easy job. First, there is no proper billeting for the troops and their accommodation is in makeshift buildings. It is a non-family station and all ranks live a life not different from what the army undergoes in operational and border areas. Unlike the international border where the regular army continues to be deployed, there is no classical and traditional "enemy". But the "threats" are plenty for the saplings—lack of water, heavy wind and shifting sand, pests like white ants, and grazing animals, to name a few. Each threat is countered by appropriate measures and the men, who are all desert dwellers from Rajasthan, are fully in synchrony with the ecological realities. Some of the conclusions that emerged after the field visit are:

(a) The unit has operated in the desert for over three decades. It has developed a unique ethos and work culture. It is unlikely that any private contractor or government department can match this ecological professionalism. Areas handed over by the ETF to civil administration had abundant wildlife and sufficient tree cover, including clumps of trees.

(b) The regimental system of the Infantry has proven itself in general and limited wars and counterinsurgency. The same ethos of the regional troops of Rajputana Rifles was visible in the ETF. Soldiers being from the region with rural background is essential. Due to cultural practices, troops have great love for nature and wildlife. This bond is evidently the core competency of the ETF. The JCOs and Senior NCOs (on Extra Regimental Establishment from fighting formations and units) had transformed into great ecologists. Unlike unpopular fatigues of working parties which soldiers have to perform in their active career, here was a totally different ethos and motivation to look after ecology. Critics who say that JCOs lack initiative may change their opinion after visiting an ETF. Perhaps this model could be a case study in leadership for the army.

(c) Unlike regular units where officers, JCOs and ORs have operational experience and tactical acumen is a function of rank or seniority, in ETF the reverse is the case. Jawans who retire from the regular army after getting selected are embodied for eight to eleven months in a year. They either serve for fifteen years or retire again when they attain the age of 55 years. On an average a jawan serves for a decade on this job. These old hands have practical experience in planting, survival and other nuances related to ecological tasks. Officers and JCOs on the contrary only serve for one or two tenures. Thus, like the proverbial "siting of an LMG" the vast repertoire of oral and practical knowledge which the soldiers have, which is much superior to what the officer may have, needs to be recognised by policy planners. Ecologists call it traditional ecological knowledge or TEK. An officer or JCO must therefore learn the trade from the lowest level. He has no Junior Command Course equivalent or an army institute to master this art. This human resource of jawans of the ETF needs to be recognised as a national asset and given its due importance in society. They can, for example, undergo some scientific courses or be granted a diploma equivalent to get accredited, to enable them to become consultants in ecological restoration projects either to corporate India or to initiate the Anna Hazare model of Ralegaon Sidhi in their villages.[11]

(d) A desert ecosystem is necessary for biodiversity. Planners in urban centres think only of food security (meaning food grains like wheat and rice) and the need to have more cereals, and so on. Water-intensive crops like rice or sugarcane become the real cash crops, thus degrading the land and using massive "virtual water". Animal husbandry is about 25 per cent of agriculture. The bulk of the landless poor survive on goats and sheep economy. Common property resources like grazing lands support a substantial part of goats and sheep. A substantial amount of the mutton economy of the country is based on the desert ecosystem. Camels, wild plants and wildlife can thrive only if we look after the desert ecosystem. Many medicinal plants grow in the desert. In Kumaon and Garhwal Himalayas local greed fuelled by corporate India has led to extinction of many wild fruits and medicinal plants; it can happen in the desert too. With the command area of the canal encroaching and blocking this area and more grazing lands coming under fencing, desert grazing land and the pastoralists are being ignored and forced to fend for themselves. Another threat is the thirst for land, including that for urbanisation. Like elsewhere in India, excess agricultural land may fall in a few hands using benami strategy. These issues need to be highlighted to bring about a holistic ecological policy.

Ecological Issues that may Impact Security

Desertification

Deserts also have a place in Nature. They play a role and support a variety of biodiversity, including herbal plants necessary for humankind. However, desertification of arable land or spread of desert is undesirable. The *Gazetteer of India Volume V*, 1973, noted about Thar desert: "the desert is advancing 800 metres a year on a broad front of 1600 km towards Ganga Plains etc." Researchers at CAZRI could not answer my query whether this was true, but later CAZRI clarified in a communication:

> In brief, the earlier view that the desert was creeping towards Delhi was found untenable. However, land degradation both within the arid lands and along its fringes are getting accentuated due to human pressures, even though the climate during the last fifty years did not worsen. The issues are complex and have been discussed in the reprints.[12]

Soil degradation is a major reason for desertification. Soil may get degraded due to faulty agricultural and irrigation practices, by water and wind erosion. Irrigation without proper drainage in an arid region can lead to waterlogging and salination. It also leads to spread of vector-borne diseases like malaria.

Indira Gandhi Canal

Greening of the desert leads to levelling off of sand dunes. Some sand dunes remain in the area of Sam, which are open to international tourism. Sand dunes in their majestic best may also exist inside the military field firing ranges such as in Mahajan (near Suratgarh) and Lathi (near Pokhran). Barmer district may also have some dunes.

There has been considerable debate on the advantages and disadvantages of Indira Gandhi canal.[13] The greening around Pokhran and Mahajan field firing ranges is a striking change. But the change from nomadic to settled agriculture brings with it socio-agricultural problems. The lifestyle and culture of traditional desert dwellers dependent on arid agriculture now changes to that of settled farmers not unlike those in southern Punjab. This generates the narrative of a dominant landed gentry with a propensity for resource capture, lower-caste or poor landless agricultural workers, the marginalised Scheduled Castes (SCs) or Other Backward Classes (OBCs) of the caste system of pastoralists and the spread of urbanisation and its consumerist values. The worst hit by this "creative destruction" would be the pastoralists. While identifying tensions may be easy, its peaceful resolution is a challenge of governance.

Pastoralists

The shrinking common property resources (CPR) and grasslands for pastoralists are giving rise to new problems. The pastoralists are mostly from the Raika and Ribari tribes. An important relationship has existed between agriculture and animal husbandry in rain-fed areas. When there was no standing crop, the farmers would welcome the large herds of sheep or cattle to graze in their fields simply for manure and urine fertilising their fields,[14] in addition to allowing the herders to graze in their forests. But now the herders are unwelcome. The better-off farmers can get chemical fertilisers in the market far more easily than sheep manure from camping pastoralists.[15] Unlike Darfur, fortunately our societal context is different and there are democratic mechanisms at work. But this issue cannot be ignored as more land is plotted for agriculture in the future and restrictions on grazing grow.

The changing pattern of land use, rapid expansion of the irrigated area and privatisation of tenancy are some of the factors responsible for erosion of livelihood security of pastoral people.[16] One estimate is that there are 20 to 22 lakh nomads constituting 10 per cent of the population of Rajasthan. In one study on the changing views of the mobile Raika pastoralists it has been shown that the state social services are designed for the sedentary population and the nomads are often unable to gain access to education, health and jobs.[17]

The government allots 5 hectares of land per household as "murba" (agricultural plots) along the command of the canal. The allottees fence off their land. Forest land under the Forest Department is also fenced off to ward off ruminants. To compound the problem, grasslands of the CPR variety are degraded.

Stall-fed cattle is not a solution because the pastoralists are mostly landless, surviving on grazing land by migration according to seasons. This is a centuries-old phenomenon. In the industrialised countries, a portion of agricultural land is set aside for fodder for stall-feeding. Some areas of well-to-do Punjab also follow this practice. But in rain-fed areas, even where arable land is available, the farmers do not find it economical to devote land exclusively for fodder production. The general practice is to feed the animals with agricultural residue.[18]

The "scientific" explanation for land degradation is grazing resorted to by graziers, forgetting that animal stock is an integral part of agriculture. It is estimated that almost 18 million people in India derive their livelihood from livestock.[19] Planners and policymakers perceive land as just a means for production of cereal crops. In the arid regions or in rain-fed India, marginal, subsistence farmers and the landless subsist on livestock as a back-up. No policy planner should overlook this reality. The saying "he is looking for greener pastures" is ignored in modernisation. The grasslands are ignored and we do not empathise with the herders' need for greener pastures. Most of the goats and sheep of Rajasthan are of the nomadic variety. A study by the Centre for Science and Environment shows that the ban on grazing on Forest Department land has also created problems for Raika camel-herders. The camel population has fallen from 0.7 million in 1992 to 0.049 million in 2003. Illegal slaughter could also be a reason for this decline.[20] Media reports now speak of rising camel prices due to demand for their milk and as draught animals to replace tractors (over 40% decline of the camel population has been reported from Jaisalmer and Barmer districts).[21]

Grazing lands have declined by 9 to 30 per cent during the second half of the twentieth century.[22] The neglect of pastoralists is not an exclusively Indian phenomenon. In the Changthan plateau of Tibet or Ladakh the Chinese are encouraging sedentarisation and are forcing conversion of grassland to settled agriculture.

One study by CAZRI of Raika graziers near Jodhpur reveals that nearly half of them practise long-duration (8 to 10 months) migration with their herds to Madhya Pradesh, Uttar Pradesh and Haryana, but less than 90 per cent of them want allocation by government of some fixed grazing areas to avoid long-distance migration. Shrinking grazing resources and changing social conditions are inducing many graziers to shift to occupations such as wage labour, petty business, etc.[23] Another finding of a CAZRI study of 2004 was that joint families had higher migration than nuclear ones. The majority of the pastoralists perceived that grazing resources deteriorated due to poor rainfall and cutting trees from grazing land, but few perceived excessive grazing as the cause of degradation.[24]

The Clash of State with Settled Farmers

At a larger level the conflict over land and water, as seen in say the Punjab, is also creeping in the converted areas of the desert, a direct fallout of the interstate water dispute between

Punjab and Rajasthan. The 1981 agreement among Punjab, Haryana and Rajasthan reallocated the Ravi-Beas waters, giving Rajasthan 8.6 million acre feet (MAF), but till such time as Rajasthan did not take its share (pending completion of the IG Canal), Punjab would take the share. This is yet another emerging security challenge due to the conflict arising from the release of water to farmers in the command zone for multiple cropping, including sowing of water-intensive crops. The infrastructure for transfer of water to the tail end of the IGNP or phase II of the project is not yet complete. Pending completion of phase II, surplus water was provided to farmers of northern Rajasthan, who have come to assume plentiful supply of water for multiple cropping and will not countenance its reduction. It is like reducing salaries in a time of inflation. Since 2005 the agitation by farmers of the phase I project in Sriganganagar, Hanumangarh and Bikaner districts has intensified over demand for release of canal water as in the past. The agitation surfaces each year at the time of sowing the Rabi wheat crop in autumn. There is also reduced flow of water on account of changed precipitation due to climate change and clogging of canals by silt or water hyacinth.

Augmentation of water supply by watershed management by way of suitable tree plantation and demand management by weaning away farmers from the lure of water-intensive crops are the new challenges to be overcome by education and awareness building. As we shall see in Chapter 5, ETF deployed in the Sutlej watershed in Himachal Pradesh indirectly is helping in maintaining the water budget.

Border, Border Fencing and Wildlife Preservation

On the borders with Pakistan and Bangladesh, the Border Security Force (BSF) is responsible for border management. Fencing of the India-Pakistan border has been completed. The border region north of Mohangarh has good wildlife. The BSF is indirectly helping in wildlife preservation by greening its location, like any unit of the Indian Army. Since the last shooting-war with Pakistan in 1971 the border has been tranquil. The army will only get deployed in a shooting-war, which current theories of international relations indicate is unlikely to happen.

Fencing and its relation to ecology brings to mind a story during the partition of India as recorded by India's great wildlife conservationist, E.P. Gee:

> When Hindus in Pakistan were moving across the new border into India, and some Muslims were leaving India to settle in Pakistan, wild animals were also not without an instinctive wish for peaceful survival. A lot of nilgai in Pakistan crossed over into India where they could be safe, and numbers of wild pigs crossed into Pakistan for their security.[25]

History seems to be repeating itself.[26] Before the fencing could be completed, the wild boar population migrated in numbers to Pakistan and in the reverse direction came many nilgais (black bull) to the Indian side! How wildlife responds to human actions has amply demonstrated, time and again, that nature has given strong instincts and the faculty of communication[27] to all living beings, not man alone. A humbling thought for the human race in its quest for conquest of Nature.

Conclusions

From this study of the Thar desert one can confidently say that the need to carry out afforestation is extremely important. But forest land should not alone be the focus. Areas where there is waterlogging and salinisation need to be approached for redress on a war footing. Commercial agriculture, and high expectations of supply of irrigation water if not met, will result in more violence and tensions. These issues need to be addressed before they fester. Ignoring the herders and pastoralists could lead to internal security problems. Leaving them to the market forces may result in our losing our biodiversity. Importantly, sufficient focus needs to be given to regeneration of CPR. Kanchan Chopra and S.C. Gulati in their study have shown that:

> (I)n the arid and semi-arid regions of India, a large part of out-migration is because of push factors such as environmental degradation and shrinkages of common property resources. The system clearly reveals that distress outmigration from rural tracts in the semi-arid and arid regions can be contained by regeneration of forests and pastureland, improving irrigation potential and bringing more land under common property regime.[28]

Taking this economic analysis as a theoretical framework may suit our planners well. Where the ETF is concerned, it may also be organised to take on the challenge of CPR and to help in stopping out-migration. Indirectly, besides helping in reviving wildlife, the ETF will help in preserving our biodiversity of livestock.

APPENDIX 1

HISTORY OF RAISING OF 123 ETF

Col K. Shardul Singh (Retd), the first Commanding Officer of 123 ETF, whom I met on 17 February 2007, recalls how one day, after having commanded an infantry battalion he was posted to command the newly raised 123 ETF. The Rajasthan main canal was having a problem of getting clogged with shifting sand dunes. Shelter-belt and sand dune stabilisation was considered essential. In the 1980s the Minister of State for Defence was Shri (Brigadier) K.P. Singh Deo (himself a Territorial Army officer) chose the Bikancr-based Grenadiers TA infantry as the initial nucleus for this raising. Later the ETF became a part of Rajputana Rifles. Col Shardul Singh was selected as he belonged to Rajasthan, though he admits that he has no formal training in ecology, forestry and the like for which the ETF was being raised. In the initial phases they stayed in tents at RD 800 in Bikaner district. The task was greening the belt south of the canal. The area also was waterlogged, which was taken care of by planting eucalyptus trees as vertical/biological drainage. Sewan grass was another species which was locally suitable. By far the most difficult tree to plant and ensure survival was the kejri. He recalled the local Rajasthani names of other trees/species that were planted—fog, peel, jugal, sarkanda and sariya. He was very proud of the achievement of his troops. He now felt that though the ETF has leapfrogged to its new location for afforestation, the real problem which it must battle is salinisation and waterlogging. He was certain that this task was more challenging and crucial than simple afforestation.

APPENDIX 2

TYPES OF PLANTS PLANTED

Un-Command Area

Common Name		*Botanical Name*
Israeli Babool	—	Acacia Tortlis
Khejri	—	Prosopsis Cinarira
Angrezi Babool	—	Prosopsis Juliflora
Parkin Sonia	—	Parkin Sonia
Rohira	—	Techomela Undulata

Command Area

Neem	—	Azadircta Indica
Siris	—	Zalbizia Lebeck
Aradu	—	Ailnthus Excelsa
Su Babool	—	Leucenia Lucocephla
Shisham	—	Dalburgia Sisso
Ber	—	Ziziphus Mauritiana
Desi Babool	—	Acacia Niltica
Sawan grass	—	Laisurus Sindicus
Safeda	—	Eucalyptus Camaldulensis

Fruit Trees with English Names

Aam	—	Mango
Grafted Ber	—	Ber
Shehtoot	—	Mulberry
Anjeer	—	Fig
Khajoor	—	Dates palm
Amrud	—	Guava
Anar	—	Pomegranate
Amla	—	Emblica Oficincus
Nimbu	—	Lemon
Kinu	—	G—orange

Source: Chart displayed in the office of the Commanding Officer.

NOTES

1. R.S. Mertia *et al.*, *Impact of Shelterbelts in Arid Regions of Western Rajasthan*, Director, Central Arid Zone Research Institute, Jodhpur, December 2006, p. 1.
2. Introduction to Convention to Combat Desertification (CCD) of UNEP and UN CCD, at <http://www.unccd.int/>, accessed 24 November 2007.
3. *Ibid.*
4. Mertia *et al.*, *Impact of Shelterbelts in Arid Regions of Western Rajasthan*, n. 1, p. 3.
5. Deepak Apte (Principal Investigator), Seminar Proceedings of Indian Army Green Governance, organised by BNHS and 12 Corps, 26 to 28 August 2004. I am thankful to Col Prakash Tewari of the Ecological Cell at Army HQ for making these proceedings available to me during my interaction with him in August 2005. Also see Rushikesh Chavan, "Southern Command Gears up to Conserve Nature", *Indian Army Green Governance* web page of BNHS website.
6. Rishad Naoroji, *Birds of Prey of India*, New Delhi: Om Books, 2006, pp. 82–3.
7. Ban Ki Moon, "A Climate Culprit in Darfur", *Washington Post*, 16 June 2007. I am thankful to Dr Kalyanaraman for bringing this piece to my notice.
8. Interview with the first Commanding Officer is at Appendix 1.
9. Lt Col R.K. Palta, "Greening the Thar", *Sainik Samachar*, 1-15 November 2006: 14-15.
10. 127 ETF has won a number of national- and state-level awards. Demographer Ashish Bose, when he visited the unit in 2003, wrote, "I could see for myself how harsh the environment was in the Thar desert: only the army with its command and control system, military discipline, a high level of physical fitness and mission commitment could take up this challenge of fighting massive environmental degradation." See Ashish Bose, "Stalling the March of Thar Desert", *Economic and Political Weekly*, 26 April 2003: 1630–2.
11. Anna Hazare retired as a Naik from the Army. Using his meagre savings as a corpus he transformed his native village at Ralegaon Sidhi in the dry region of Ahmadnagar district of Maharashtra to an ecologically sound self-sustaining village, using simple techniques such as rainwater harvesting.
12. Reply of e-mail to Director CAZRI of 3 March 2007 by Dr Amar Kar, Principal Scientist & Head, Division of Natural Resources & Environment, Central Arid Zone Research Institute, Jodhpur. I am thankful to CAZRI for sending the report at note 1. The reprints quoted are the annual highlights of research of 2003, 2004 and 2005.

These valuable reports are available on the net. See <www.cazri.res.in>.

13. B.G. Verghese, *Winning the Future,* New Delhi: Centre for Policy Research/Konark, 1994. The author has devoted to the theme a chapter titled "A Desert Brought to Life", pp. 41–74. For excessive irrigation and poor drainage leading to waterlogging and salinity, see P.S. Vijay Shankar, "Unlocking the Hidden Potential of Dryland Agriculture", *Seminar,* No. 564 (August 2006): 16–19. For a fascinating account affecting endemic raptor population and decline of vultures, see Naoroji, *Birds of Prey of India,* n. 6, pp. 57, 82–3. The author attributes the drop in Egyptian vultures to the reduction in the number of Rebaris or the wandering tribes of Rajasthan. In earlier times when many Rebaris used to operate, the vultures depended on the waste food and faecal matter of the sheep, camels, etc.
14. V.K. Madhavan, "From Guar and Bajra to Apples and Cauliflower", *Seminar,* No. 564 (August 2006): 44–7.
15. Arun Agrawala and Vasant K. Saberwal, "Raika Pastoralists in Rajasthan", *Seminar,* No. 564 (August 2006): 30–4.
16. "Experts Call for Recognition of Rajasthan as a Pastoral Region", *The Hindu* (New Delhi), 25 November 2007.
17. Agrawala and Saberwal, "Raika Pastoralists in Rajasthan", n. 15.
18. The importance of fodder is well appreciated by our dryland subsistence farmers. Often fodder yield is considered more crucial than grain yield. See Rajeshwari Raina, "Researching the Drylands", *Seminar,* No. 564 (August 2006): 25-9.
19. Government of India, *Report of the Working Group on Animal Husbandry and Dairying, Tenth Five Year Plan (2002—2007),* New Delhi: Planning Commission, 2002, as quoted by Sagri R. Ramdas and Nitya S. Ghotge, "India's Livestock Economy", *Seminar,* No. 564 (August 2006): 20-4.
20. Arnab Pratim Dutta, "Raika's raison d'etre: Ban on grazing pushes the pastoral community to disappearance", *Down to Earth,* 31 March 2007: 27.
21. *The Hindu* (New Delhi), 29 April 2008.
22. CAZRI, Summary of Research, Major Achievements, p. 3, at <http://www.cazri.res.in/Achievements(main).htm>, accessed March 2007.
23. CAZRI, *Highlight of Research,* 2003, p. 9.
24. CAZRI, *Highlight of Research,* 2004, pp. 6-7. One author has even challenged the notion that goats and sheep are a major cause of deforestation. He blames it on man's mismanagement rather than to an inherent fault of the animals. See S. Chandra, "Anticipating a Spurt in International Trade", Sheep and Goat Section, *The Hindu Survey of Agriculture,* 2002, pp. 151–7.

25. E.P. Gee, *The Wild Life of India,* London: Collins, 1964, p. 109.
26. I am grateful to a BSF official for sharing this fascinating story with me. He had been a witness to it while posted at a border outpost on the India–Pakistan border. Lt Gen R.K Gaur(Retd), in a slide show on Ladakh at the India International Centre on 17 January 2009 showed how wild asses called Skyang have fled to Ladakh from Chinese occupied Tibet as the Han Chinese eat the animal.
27. Fritjof Capra in *The Web of Life* (1997) alludes to the fact that even bacteria perceive certain characteristics of their environment. They sense chemical differences in their surroundings and accordingly swim towards sugar and away from acid; they sense and avoid heat, and so on. According to Humberto Maturana's study of consciousness, communication is not transfer of information, but rather a coordination of behaviour between living organisms.
28. Kanchan Chopra and S.C. Gulati, *Migration, Common Property Resources and Environmental Degradation: Interlinkages in India's Arid and Semi-arid Regions,* New Delhi: Sage, 2001, p. 66.

Camel Family Happily Browsing on Trees Planted By ETF.

Rohira Trees Planted Near the Battalion Headquarters.

Medicinal Plants Like these Under Threat.

Commanding Officer with Self Created Nursery of *Ber* Trees Ready for Plantation.

Offtake of Channel from Canal for Watering of Plants.

4

The Kumaon Region

Pithoragarh, Almora and Ranikhet

Brief History

130 Infantry Battalion (TA) Ecological at Pithoragarh in Kumaon hills of Uttarakhand, which I visited from 28 to 30 May 2007, was raised in 1994. The driving force behind its raising was the then Chief of the Army Staff, the late General P.C. Joshi, who hailed from the region. Ecological work needed to be done in the area and sufficient population of ex-servicemen could be embodied for the job. The Pithoragarh region is the nursery of many soldiers, mostly in the Kumaon Regiment. As in any other hill area, soldiering is a dominant profession in the region. Because of low industrialisation and urbanisation jobs are limited, leading to migration and the so-called money order economy.

This unit was a two-company ETF affiliated to the Kumaon Regiment till April 2008. Two additional companies have since been raised. It is composed of ex-servicemen hailing from the region, thus giving an inherent advantage of traditional ecological knowledge (TEK) of the troops. During 1995-2000 (I Project) the ETF successfully afforested 2749 hectares in Dharchula (north of Pithoragarh) region by planting 34.10 lakh plants. This period also included afforestation in and around Pithoragarh Cantonment. In the Kamakhya Hill Ridge (overlooking the military hospital) 1,19,500 trees were planted in 1995-96 in an area of 70 hectares. In 1999, 25,000 trees were planted in 11 hectares on RR Hill. The greening of Pithoragarh cantonment and the creation of ecological park-cum-golf course has been the work of 130 ETF.

In Project II, a six-year cycle from 2000 to 2006, 130 ETF afforested 3251 hectares, planting 29.46 lakh plants in the Kali Ganga watershed east of Pithoragarh on the features astride roads Nainipatal-Lacher-Mar-Manle and Munakot-Jhulakhet-Kuseri-Arkani-Mar (see sketch). Project III is in progress since 2006 in the Ram Ganga watershed. Five hundred hectares have been planted with 4.5 lakh plants in 2006-7. The two companies (named as M and K companies) are now afforesting another 500 hectares. M company is operating astride axis Salmora, in areas north-west of Pithoragarh near villages Bahuri Gaon, Bunga Chhina and Sil (see sketch). K company is operating south of Pithroragarh on axis Rora, Jakh, Puran and Balkot.

Uniqueness of the Region

Land Does Not Belong to the Forest Department

The area being afforested in not degraded land owned by the Forest Department. It is village land owned by the locals, which also include common property resources (CPR). Thus, in a way, the Forest Department is a competitor. The ETF has to locate, motivate and then convince the locals and village(s) Panchayat(s) to get an area afforested and project sanctioned. This demands a high level of military civil inter-relations. As a rule the area selected is the toughest for physical accessibility and ecologically challenging. As part of the project the locals need to be convinced to avoid a particular area for grazing till the yield becomes sustainable after afforestation. The land identified for afforestation may be abandoned terraced farms or degraded CPR or open access barren patches (see photographs). Only ecologically suitable trees are being planted. These include trees which provide fodder, fuel, fruit, and medicinal value. All efforts are made to allow natural growth to flourish. The locals in some areas were of the view that roots which existed before terraced fields were cut would also grow naturally over a period of time. With afforestation though theoretically the arable land may reduce, the ecological benefit of afforestation in the long term would outweigh the loss. It will also facilitate better animal husbandry as sufficient nutrients as grass will be available for grazing. Broad-leaved trees will provide the much-needed ecological services including recharge of ground water, nutrient recycling and reviving the perennial springs and improve the micro-climate.

Theoretical Framework for A Better Understanding of Ecological Degradation and Its Cure

Three important questions need to be answered when undertaking ecological restoration:

(1) How does one measure ecological degradation?
(2) What are the causes of ecological degradation in the Himalayas?
(3) How can one regenerate the degradation? For measurement, remote sensing is a powerful tool to establish the degree of degradation. Also, people who live in the area over time provide anecdotal evidence on the changes in rainfall pattern, deforestation and loss of biodiversity.

The traditional Theory of Himalayan Degradation (THED) suggests that anthropogenic or accelerated erosion is a serious problem in the steep-sloped and fragile natural environment of the Himalayan region. It argues that land degradation is driven by population growth, increased number of livestock, and inefficient local agricultural techniques.[1] It was believed that over-use by local farmers and pastoralists threatened fragile mountain and river environment. This understanding led governments to strictly curtail traditional land-use practices. This may be called the "expert-led policy model". In this, the results of scientific study are treated as authoritative and apolitical. Policy accordingly is framed. Since the 1980s scholars began questioning the science of this policy. The other model, called "political and discursive", has a much broader knowledge foundation of policy. In a more democratic system, besides powerful and wealthy people who stand to gain, there are many other voices of small farmers, social movements and so on, which have an effective role in shaping policy.

A research article on Nepal on the need to regenerate terraced fields which have been degraded due to out-migration of village labour force is relevant here.[2] In the old THED, rapid conversion of forest land to agriculture on mountain slopes was considered an important cause of environmental degradation and poverty in Nepal. This theory was challenged. It was shown that forests in hills and mountain areas have remained more or less intact, despite population growth after the 1950s. Further, the positive impact on geomorphic process due to modification of hill slopes for agricultural use through terrace construction and runoff management by local farmers was highlighted.[3] The paper highlighted that large areas of agricultural land were being left idle, resulting in geomorphic damage like that due to landslide. Farmland abandonment does not automatically lead to plant colonisation. The authors suggested, "Careful land management is necessary even after abandonment to minimise adverse geomorphic and ecological consequences." Here in Pithoragarh, the ETF was performing just this type of work. Both Nepal and India face this common challenge and much can be learnt from this Indian experience. Full credit must be given to the local government and the ETF in undertaking this important task of regenerating abandoned terraced fields. Why this is important is that Nepal Himalayas also suffers similar problems of fragmentation of land as in India. What the study shows is that careful land management is necessary with new opportunities to develop commercial dairy. Probably the problem in Nepal is more acute as it was also torn by an insurgency for a decade. The ETF model of the Indian Army can be suitably adapted in Nepal by employing former insurgents. This is covered in Chapter 8 on military-to-military cooperation.

Ecological Degradation is More Pronounced in Almora and Ranikhet

Recent work of R. Prabhakar et al. shows that in the eastern half of Uttarakhand 61 per cent of forests have less than 40 per cent crown cover. It shows how satellite image interpretation is never free of error and how forest degradation is considerably understated.[4] Even without remote sensing technology it is easy to notice indicators of environmental degradation such as barren hills, absence of springs or flows in rivers, loss of vegetation and hand-pumps without any water. While travelling from the foothills of Kumaon on the north-south axis Tanakpur-Champavat-Pithrogarh, along the road one encountered mostly broad-leaved trees. The forests were mostly mixed. The areas on the axis in Champavat and Pithoragarh were green with more number of broad-leaved trees. At Champavat, the people appeared to be very proud of their healthy forests. In contrast, monoculture and ecological degradation was more visible and pronounced as one travelled west. While returning from Pithoragarh to Ranikhet via Almora it was noticed that the rivers were nearly dry and at most a trickle. Environmental degradation was clearly visible.[5] Most of the hand-pumps were dry though pre-monsoon rains had been regular in 2007. The hills were either barren or covered with a variety of monoculture of pines. During the colonial period, the British encouraged pines for turpentine and log wood, eliminating the local species like oak and deodar. Thus in Kumaon due to the need for wood for strategic needs such as railway sleepers and ships, pine monoculture was undertaken by the British. Many areas in the Kumaon and elsewhere are covered with pine.[6]

The ecological ills of excess of monoculture pines have been written about.[7] Ramachandra Guha has shown that within the major division between conifers and broad-leaved species, the most important and common species, especially in the altitudes inhabited by human population are the banj or Ban oak (Quercus incana) and the chir or chil pine (pinus roxburghii). In general, species distribution reflects the process of ecological succession whereby stable forest cover is established in any terrain. The succession is in three stages—

(i) *Initial stage*: certain species of trees, usually with small or light seed take possession of newly exposed ground;

(ii) *Transitional stage*: changes on ground already clothed with some vegetative cover; and

(iii) The *climax stage* towards a hydrophilous (*i.e.*, adapted to plentiful water supply) type of vegetation which the locality is capable of supporting.[8] Guha made two important points. First, in the Himalayas, the oaks and other broad-leaved species represent stage (iii) and the conifers stage (ii). In the days before forest management mixed forests were the norm. While oak and other broad-leaved species are more valuable for hill agriculture, on both ecological and economic grounds the conifers have had, since the inception of "scientific management", a variety of commercial uses. The second point observed was that while "progressive succession" from stage (i) to (iii) occurs in Nature, "retrogressive" succession from stage (iii) to (ii) to (i) can be caused by the hand of man, either accidentally or deliberately.

Commercial gains via the Forest Department's revenue with pine-related products could be one powerful incentive for the state government to maintain the status quo much against the principles of forest policy to balance ecology. It is an ecological challenge how to replace monoculture pine forests with ecologically suitable trees on a massive scale in Kumaon. The objective of this should be to facilitate water and nutrients recycling. Sufficient knowledge now exists that mixed forests suitable to a particular ecology and micro-climate are the best solution for a healthy ecology. A programme on a war footing needs to be undertaken keeping ETF as the basic structure to undertake this task.[9] The people of Kumaon are known to be politically aware, but somehow it appears that they have resigned to the fate of an entire region being intruded by ecologically harmful monoculture pine. This challenge needs to be tackled head on and it is hoped that policy planners now begin to address it. For a beginning re-entrants and former groves near springs and water channels may be reforested, removing pines. If this experiment works it may gain momentum by its demonstrative power.

The foothill cities of Haldwani and Kathgodam are expanding as new urban areas. Here informally it was learnt that people living in the region have observed reduction in river runoff over time and think that hydroelectric projects are of no use as the rivers are mostly in lean flow. This partly anecdotal observation has its own value and lessons. Later, when travelling from the foothills of the Shivaliks from Pathankot to Dharamsala (covered in Chapter 5) in Kangra in the Beas watershed, lush green broad-leaved forests were the norm with good local rains. The locals in Dharamsala who experience rain virtually every day were waiting for a few more years to beat Cherrapunji's record of the highest rainfall in India (11 metres). Though this is a local phenomenon, it underlines the importance of mixed forests in keeping the micro-rainfall cycle.

Other Intrusive Species which May Pose a Long-term Ecological Threat

Another ubiquitous threat to ecology is the spread of intrusive species. Lantana and congress grass (Parthenium) were noticed at a number of places in the Kumaon region. Not many are aware of the threat. For a beginning, an ETF type of organisation is needed to remove these intrusive species. But the military alone cannot overcome this problem. The entire society needs to be mobilised, beginning with inclusion of grassroots ecological issues in school and National Cadet Corps (NCC) curriculum.

Conclusion

The ecological challenges being faced by Kumaon Himalayas will take a long time to overcome. Besides afforestation of fallow land and CPR, as is being done with great devotion by the ETF, this field visit helped in identifying problems of ecological degradation such as the need for removal of the ubiquitous chir pines and intrusive species. All is not well with the Kumaon Himalayan ecosystem. No amount of development by way of laying roads will be successful if the ecology by way of afforestation and reforestation is not taken care of. With the youth tending to shun agriculture, there is also a chance of traditional ecological knowledge being forgotten. It is for the devoted ex-servicemen of the region to come to grips with the challenge and assist the administration in ecological restoration of the Kumaon Himalayas.

NOTES

1. Piers Blaikie and Joshua Muldavin, "The Politics of Environmental Policy with a Himalayan Example: *Analysis from East-West Center*", No. 74, June 2004, Honolulu: East-West Center.
2. Narendra Raj Khanal and Teiji Watanbe, "Abandonment of Agricultural Land and Its Consequences: A Case Study in the Sikles Area, Gandaki Basin, Nepal", *Mountain Research and Development*, 26(1) (February 2006): 32–40.
3. *Ibid.*
4. R. Prabhakar, E. Somanathan and B.S. Mehta, "How Degraded are Himalayan Forests?", *Current Science*, 91(1) (10 July 2006).
5. Some literature of interest being Madhav Gadgil and Ramachandra Guha, *This Fissured Land: An Ecological History of India*, New Delhi: Oxford University Press, ninth impression, 2006; and Ajay S. Rawat (ed.), *History of Forestry in India*, New Delhi: Indus, 1991.
6. Pine monoculture was also prominent in eastern Himachal Pradesh. See sketch in Chapter 5.
7. Ramachandra Guha, *The Unquiet Woods: Ecological Change and Peasant Resistance in the Himalayas*, New Delhi: Oxford University Press, 2001; Madhav Gadgil and Ramachandra Guha, *This Fissured Land*, n. 5; and Bhaskar Sinha, "Introduction of the European Pines in the Himalayas and the Subsequent Environmental Degradation", Research Highlights, NISTAD, at <http://envfor.nic.in/report/0102/chapter07.html#res-gdpihed accessed on 02 June 2007>.
8. Guha, *Ibid.* (Expanded edition, Oxford India Paperbacks, 2001), pp. 37-8.
9. It is worth recalling how in the 1970s and '80s eucalyptus was planted in north India to cater for quick-growing trees mostly for pulp. Another case is the intrusive vilayati kikar which dominates tree species grown by forest departments.

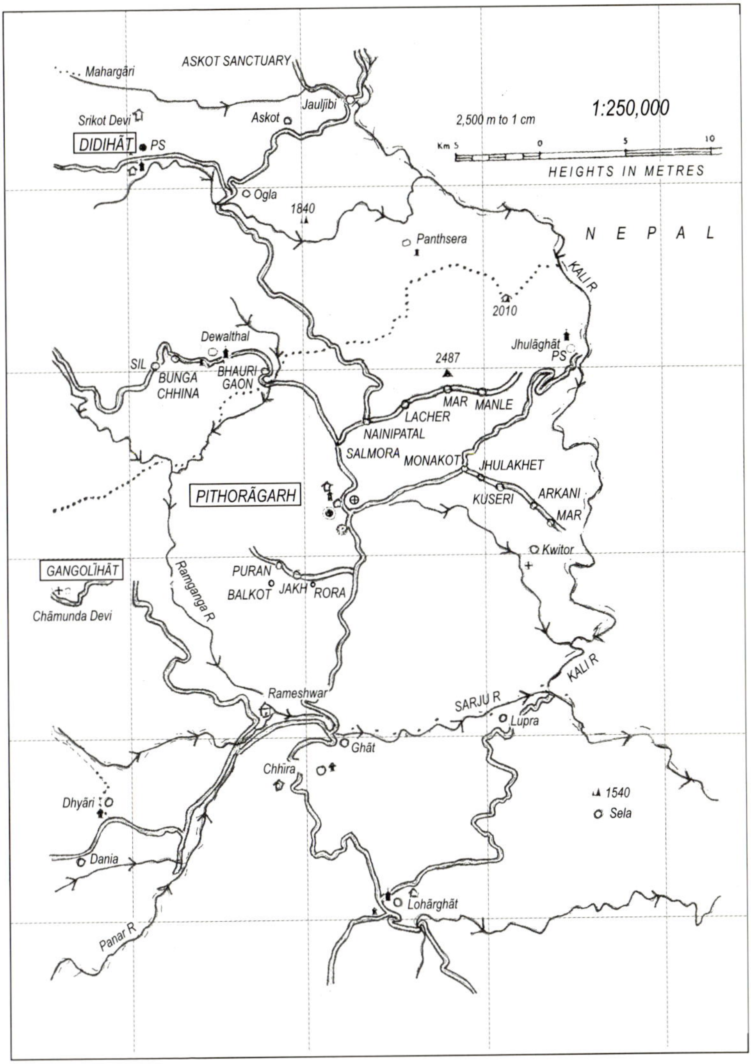

Areas Visited in and Around Pithoragarh

Common Property Resource(CPR) Mountain Top Identified for Greening for the ETF Beginning Year 2007 Near Bunga Chhina.

Terraced Abandoned Plots for Regeneration by the ETF at Jakh.

Degraded Hills Near Almora Awaiting ETF Type of Treatment for Regeneration.

5

Himachal Pradesh and Punjab

133 Infantry Battalion (TA) Ecological (a new raising), located at Tattapani, Sutlej watershed in Himachal Pradesh, was visited in June 2007. The opportunity was also utilised to study the Sutlej watershed from the ecological perspective till just short of the Sino-Indian border at Shipki La (area Khab). Sketch 5.1 shows the area of Sutlej watershed from Tattapani to Pooh. Later the Punjab and Kangra Valley were also visited.

133 Infantry Battalion The Dogra Regiment (TA) Ecological

133 ETF is fully funded by the Himachal Pradesh government. It was raised in March 2006 as a one-company ETF; by September 2006 it completed its raising. The battalion HQ is at Kufri with a company at Tattapani. The total strength of the ETF is three officers, 5 Junior Commissioned Officers (JCOs) and 139 Other Ranks (ORs). The battalion headquarters has two officers, two JCOs and 40 ORs. A company has one officer, three JCOs and 99 ORs. The raising cost is about Rs 1.2 crore.

The eligibility conditions to join the ETF are: (a) ex-servicemen from Himachal Pradesh in receipt of pension; (b) below 45 years of age for ORs and 48 years for JCOs (unlike the ETF in Rajasthan or Pithoragrah, which have serving JCOs on deputation, former JCOs are also enrolled in this ETF); (c) not a low medical category person (SHAPE1 in medical parlance); (d) within five years of release from service with character as exemplary/very good; (e) can serve up to seven years and 50 years of age for ORs and 55 years for JCOs which ever is earlier. (The Commanding Officer explained that the upper age bracket has been kept at 50 years to give more employment opportunities to the large ex-servicemen population of the region).

The task is conservation of ecology by way of afforestation and reforestation, soil conservation and allied activities and environmental awareness programmes. The ETF is deployed in area Tattapani near the Sutlej in general area Sarour and Thog on the axis along road Tattapani-Karsog (about 4 km from Tattapani). The area is akin to a remote field area and troops have to construct makeshift shelters. The trappings of a military station are non-existent. There is no provision to keep families.

The ETF has been allotted two sites of 20 hectares each of highly degraded forest land. The general work cycle or schedule of an ETF in this area, which is based on the monsoons, is as follows:

> *Preparatory work,* which is done in January-April, includes the following: (i) land allotment; (ii) reconnaissance by ETF and forest officials; (iii) barbed-wire and brushwood fencing; (iv) digging of pits and trenches; and (v) construction of check dams and harvesting ponds.

Plantation of saplings is done in the period July-October. Table 5.1 lists some variety of saplings being planted by the ETF.

Table 5.1: Variety of Saplings

Common Name	*Botanical Name*
Khair	Acacia Catechu
Robinia	Robinia Pseudoacacia
Ooe	Albizzia Stipulata
Feguda	Ficus Palmata
Amla	Emblica Officinalis
Akhrot	Walnut-Juglansregia
Biyul	Grewia Optiva
Shisham	Dalbergia Sissoo
Kachnar	Bauhinia Purpurea
Sahtoot	Morus Alba
Dadu	Punica Gratum
Tuni	Cedral Toona
Kenth	Pyrus Pasha
Aam	Mangifera Indica

Source: Briefing inputs by 133 ETF.

Disembodiment. Being TA units it is mandatory for the troops to be disembodied during the lean period May-June and November-December.

Aftercare includes replanting of saplings. The Headquarters of the ETF being located at Kufri close to the state capital Shimla is also in the task of environmental awareness programme by organising van mahotsav (forest festival), supply of fodder to locals and education of schoolchildren on ecology-related tasks.

Challenges and Area-specific Issues

Civil-Military Relations. In Tattapani the ex-servicemen population is not in abundance. Most of the troops from Himachal Pradesh hail from traditional regions like Kangra and its neighbourhood. This low population of ex-servicemen poses a unique challenge to the ETF in generating good civil-military relations and institutionalising afforestation with the cooperation of the locals. Only after three to five years would the results be visible. A subsistence grazier may not grasp the long-term ecological benefits of afforestation and the rich fodder that it would generate in the future when he compares it with the restriction on his movement due to fencing. The concept of common property resource (CPR) and resource use (in scarcity conditions) may it be for temporary camps for the ETF, use of common water resources or grazing ground for goats and sheep are common challenges faced by the ETF. With deep ecological understanding and decades of experience gained, ETF is capable of demonstrating greater transparency and sincerity. This in turn would generate a groundswell of positive public opinion in favour of more ETFs in other regions. The need to serve the ecology in the ultimate analysis is dependent on the political leadership of the state who are ready to release funds much against forest and civilian bureaucracy's vested interests. Thus winning over the ecological trust of the locals is as important as survival of trees. Being the first ETF in the state, 133 ETF has the potential to be the pioneers on the restoration of Himalayan ecology by way of the ETF. The Dogra Regiment and ex-servicemen from Himachal Pradesh are ecologically connected to the region. Their potential is waiting to be explored through the time-tested regimental system of the Indian Army.

Project Affected People. The Kol dam is being constructed downstream by the National Thermal Power Corporation (NTPC). The project-affected people (PAPs) are being compensated by the civil administration, but livelihood issue from reduced tourism may leave some PAPs bitter. Tattapani has natural hot sulphur springs and is on the tourist circuit, including end point of river rafting. With construction of the dam, some areas may no longer be approachable for tourists. It is here that afforestation being done by the ETF may at a future date attract tourists also. The ETF with its good work and practical methods of tackling ecological problems may well be in the lead to facilitate revival of tourism at Tattapani. If possible, ETF may also offer suitable suggestions to the local authorities to maximise tourist potential. If due to unforeseen reasons there is a negative movement by the PAPs the good job done by ETF may not get its due appreciation. It is in the interest of the ETF to be sensitive to this issue.

Comparison of ETF with Forest Department. Ecological services cannot always be measured in economic or financial terms. But comparison is often asked for and even desired by policy planners. Experience so far shows that the Forest Department or the ministry feel that ETF is not cost-effective. My interaction with the three ETFs in the field trips showed, however, that the military/ETF argues that survival and the type of difficult terrain on which it performs its task is anytime more effective than had it been done by the Forest Department. This difference of perceptions is expected because of differences of organisational culture. An independent study by the military in the costing and comparative part is urgently needed to rest this problem. The Forest Department may already have data and analysis to show how its work is more cost-effective. The ETF inputs would help in preparing a proper ecological audit report and highlight the benefits of the ETF strategy.

Sutlej Watershed from Tattapani till Khab (Near the Sino-Indian Border Short of Shipki La)

The Sutlej watershed with roads (such as National Highway 22) running along the bank at most of the places is an important strategic region. Hydroelectric projects such as those at Nathpa-Jhakri region provide essential power to the northern grid. Infrastructure building is in full swing and the full hydroelectric potential of the Sutlej basin will soon be tapped, including the proposed 636 MW project at Khab just near the international border. From the ecological point of view, preservation of soil in the watershed and afforestation are important dimensions of environmental security.

In spite of the best methods used during construction,[1] roads are prone to disruption due to landslides/rockslide. Silt due to natural reasons or induced due to debris from roads is a perennial problem in retarding generation of electricity to the full potential. Dredging or shut-down has often been resorted to. Damage from the floods of August 2000 was still visible at Tattapani. The Fourth Assessment Report (4 AR) of the Intergovernmental Panel on Climate Change (IGPCC) warns that:

> Glacier melt in the Himalaya is projected to increase flooding, and rock avalanches from destabilised slopes, and to affect water resources within the next two to three decades. This will be followed by decreased river flows as the glaciers retreat.[2]

There are fears in downstream India on reduction of water flow by diversion on the Sutlej upstream by the Chinese or sudden floods due to glacier lake outflow bursts, as has been experienced because of an artificial lake formation on the Parechu river in Tibet. Recent media reports[3] indicate that a joint mechanism has been set up between India and China on exchange of vital information on the flow of the rivers flowing from China into India. It is clear that ecological restoration would be a "no regret" option. Some measures from environmental security point of view are suggested in the succeeding paragraphs.

Tree Plantation. Ecologically suitable trees would improve the micro-climate, including helping the water budget by inducing local rains and also help in soil stabilisation. Where possible, massive afforestation needs to be done.

Overcoming Ecological Problems Caused by Road Construction. One area where fresh thinking is needed is chronic landslide/rockslide along the roads built by the Border Road Organisation (BRO). A study conducted by the engineers of the Sutlej Jal Vidyut Nigam on excess silt attributes it not to the tributaries such as Spiti and Parechu which pass through erosion-prone cold desert areas of Ladakh, Spiti and Tibet but to the tonnages of debris being thrown by the state Public Works Department (PWD) and the BRO, the two main agencies involved in the construction and maintenance of roads in the region.[4] Chronic/sensitive spots where roadblocks are a routine need to be identified and ecological restoration done on the slopes. The BRO with its limited resources may not alone be able to undertake the task. At places high above the road, water channels and loose earth cascade down with the slightest disturbance. At present, the gallant bulldozer operators of the BRO clear the block as soon as it is formed, quickly reverse the dozer to avoid being hit by hurtling rocks and stones (when the look-out sentry, normally a poor migrant labourer of BRO, gives real-time information on the falling debris). It becomes an annual feature and we resign ourselves to acts of nature. Though road construction takes ecological factors into account, due to the urge to complete a job on time and limited budget, the best ecological practices may not be strictly adhered to. If a fresh ecological assessment is made, with soil stabilisation strategies on slopes, we can mitigate frequent slides. There is a need to revisit this issue from two perspectives, as under:

(a) *Roads already constructed.* Here a survey and data base would establish chronic zones of blocks. The BRO alone may not be able to resolve the problem. A mini-ETF type of organisation may have to be formed to effect soil stabilisation by planting bushes, trees and also establishing the root cause of the problem. It is visualised that in the long term this exercise would reduce the frequency and magnitude of roadblocks and would provide better mobility for military and civil traffic.

(b) *Roads to be constructed.* The National Commission on Forests notes:

> **Faulty Road Construction in Hills.** Roads are the lifelines of any development process. The fruits of development cannot reach the deprived and population residing away from the mainstream till there exists a well developed network of roads, which is eco-friendly as well. However, road construction in hilly areas is quite different from constructing roads in plains, and often results in degradation of adjoining forest areas. The situation in these areas is such that in most cases the road has to pass through the forest area. Since the resources are always scarce, effort on the part of the Public Works Department is to construct the roads at minimum cost so that the maximum area is covered. In doing so, the basic principle of two-third cutting and one-third filling is forgotten and the debris are rolled down the hill slope, which results in destruction of natural regeneration, covering the forest floor with debris making it hostile to any vegetative growth and siltation of dams down stream. Rolling down of debris also inflicts wounds to the trees, which mostly result in the drying up of a number of trees. In view of this, care has to be taken to see that the construction of roads on the hilly areas be done on scientific principles, with proper management of dumping of debris and its rehabilitation subsequently. While issuing clearance under the FCA*, the MoEF must ensure that effective conditions to prevent degradation of forests because of rolling down of debris are laid down and, still important, is the fact that the conditions laid down are effectively enforced by the State Governments and regional offices of the MoEF.[5]

---

* Forest (Conservation) Act.

Although the military by itself may not be able to ensure that the observations of the Forest Commission noted above are addressed, it must take up the issues in civil-military dialogues.

Removal of Unsuitable Trees. Some areas in the past were planted with trees as monoculture plantation that we now know are not ecologically suitable. Eucalyptus and pines are two visible examples. Some areas where monoculture exists are shown in Sketch 1. It is time that these issues are brought into focus and remedial action taken by the government department concerned. In this instance, the pines (near Solan) and eucalyptus (on Sutlej bank from Jhakri till Sainj, see Sketch) are probably the earlier initiatives of the Forest Department.

S.S. Negi has shown that Eucalyptus Sp or safeda is a native specie of Australia which now has 170 specie plantations in India. According to him, large-scale plantation in the dry valley of the Sutlej near Rampur Bushiar in Himachal Pradesh was introduced for reasons such as (a) rapid growth, (b) ease of establishment even on degraded land, and (c) simple artificial regeneration technique (natural regeneration does not take place except in patches in Rampur).[6] The utility of the tree is that the wood is hard, strong and durable, it is cheap timber for door and window frames, it is used for domestic heating and cooking, tannin is extracted from the bark, and is extremely suited for afforestation of degraded areas and wasteland.[7] The commercial aspect now needs to be reassessed against the ecological harm the tree does. Now with better knowledge and experience, these plantations can be replaced with ecologically suitable species.

The Case of Chandimandir Cantonment. The Chandimandir military area abuts the Shivaliks astride the main highway. It has massive and tall eucalyptus trees. In the past decades when such trees were part of social and farm forestry, it was not considered as ecologically harmful. But now, there is a requirement to transplant and change the corridor of the highway to ecologically suitable species. A study conducted by the Central Soil and Water Conservation Research Institute, Dehradun, shows that if eucalyptus is allowed to grow around a natural reservoir for about ten years, the water in it gets reduced by 16 per cent. If the offshoots of the same plant are again allowed to grow for another ten years the water goes down by 27 per cent. The results have indicated loss of moisture ranging from 10 to 12 per cent in the area where the eucalyptus trees are allowed to grow for more than twenty years.[8]

A study may be done and if found feasible, an ETF type of force may well undertake this transformation. As the road is visible, this job will get sufficient publicity and the initiatives of the military in restoring the environment will rightfully find their recognition. With this, future projections of ETF will surely get the support of the people and the political class.

Eastern Rivers of the Indus Basin, the Punjab and Beas Watershed

Broadly, the provisions of the Indus Water Treaty (IWT) 1960[9] are as under:

(a) Signed on 19 September 1960, but effective from 1 April 1960.
(b) The treaty fixes the rights and obligations of India and Pakistan in relation to each other concerning the use of waters of the Indus system.
(c) The waters of the eastern rivers (Ravi, Beas and Sutlej) with an average annual flow of about 33 million acre feet (MAF) stand allocated to India.
(d) The waters of the western rivers (Indus, Jhelum and Chenab) with an average annual flow of about 135 MAF largely allocated to Pakistan except certain specified uses by India.

The treaty allows with restrictions projects on the Western rivers by India. The three prominent projects under contention with Pakistan on the western rivers are Baglihar on the Chenab (about 170 km own side of LoC). Then is the Tulbul navigation lock (called Wullar barrage by Pakistan) on the Jhelum and Kishenganga project on Kishenganag (Neelam) river before it joins the Jhelum river. Due to the unfavourable political climate between both countries, most projects being unbdertaken by India have been politicised. While IWT is not being considered, but it is an important division of six rivers ignoring ecological boundaries and accepting political boundaries for dividing the waters.

Satluj Beas Ravi Development Master Plan

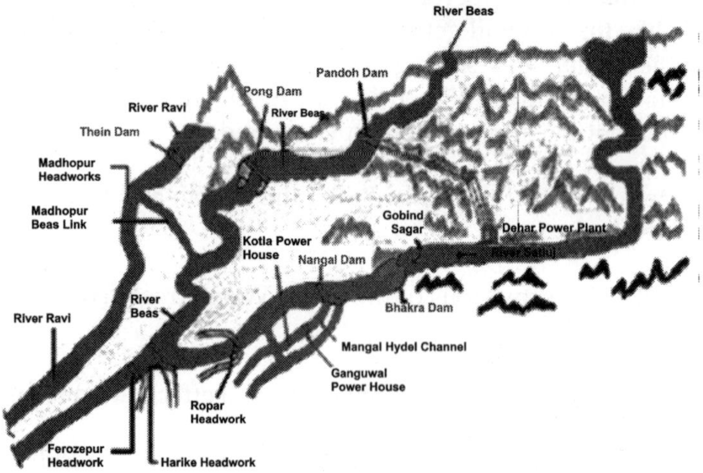

Source: Bhakra Beas Management Board, at <http://bbmb.gov.in/english/menu2.asp>.

Of the eastern rivers allocated to India, after the construction of the Ranjit Sagar dam and Shapur Kandi project on the Ravi, the losses of water which used to flow into Pakistan would end. Losses also take place because of non-maintenance of structures at Madhopur headworks and the Upper Bari Doab Canal (UBDC). India has already formulated certain schemes on the eastern rivers for prevention of loss across the international border.

There were certain problems also on the Harike headworks on the maintenance and siltation of the reservoir. Due to terrain features, before crossing into Pakistan the Ravi criss-crosses the border a number of times. Until it finally crosses into Pakistan, the waters of the Ravi belong to India. But there are a number of problems because of the criss-crossing. Similarly, the Sutlej criss-crosses the border a number of times before finally crossing over to Pakistan.[10] The four tributaries of the Ravi (Devak, Basantar, Bein and Tarnah) flow into Pakistan and carry seasonal water. India is losing a lot of water across this border. Though there is an attempt to have check dams on these tributaries, it is unlikely that water flow during the rains in the area or catchment can be stopped. It is unlikely that India will be ever be able to divert or capture all that which flows from India into the eastern rivers into Pakistan. Rather the flow continues to be an ecological bonus or service so important for the continuation of the eastern rivers when they enter Pakistan.

The principles followed in the IWT were:

(a) No interdependence. Each party free to develop the waters allotted to it.
(b) Approach the problem on functional rather than political basis.
(c) Existing uses must be continued but not necessarily from the same sources. This was the first time in history that riparian rights were accepted but not from the same source. Otherwise we could not have got the eastern rivers.

The entire development of Punjab, Haryana and Rajasthan owes it to this treaty.

Beas Watershed

Compared to the region of Almora and Ranikhet in Kumaon (see Chapter 4), the Beas watershed or the Kangra Valley area is greener, with more broad-leaved trees, more like the Champavat region of Kumaon. Not much of terraced agriculture has been done as there are natural flat valleys and doons in the region of these Shivalik hills. This is a natural advantage enjoyed by the watershed. However, this should not make us complacent and the entire watershed and catchment area need to be taken into account.

The micro-climate of Dharamsala region where the Shivaliks encounter the massive Dhauladhar ranges gives rise to the phenomenon of local rains. According to the locals the Met Department is waiting for ten-year data, when annual rain could be more than that of Cherrapunji in Meghalaya. This is good news and the impact of green broad-leaved trees is considered phenomenal for such rains. This is also the case in the Siang region of Arunachal Pradesh. We must not underestimate the contribution of ecologically suitable trees to precipitation.

The Contemporary Punjab-Malwa and Manjha

Informal conversations with war veterans revealed that in the ex-servicemen category 50 per cent or even less are still in the business of agriculture in Punjab. Most let out their land for annual rates which range from Rs 10,000 to 14,000 probably for an acre. Fragmentation of land and break-up of joint family has direct implications for livelihood. Travelling from Faridkot to Pathankot through Malwa and Majha region of the famous Bari doab areas between Ravi and Beas/Sutlej[11] one discerns that Malwa is relatively more arid than Manjha. The impact of irrigation is evident in lush fields and muti-cropping. This area of Manjha and Malwa is also the main recruiting ground of the troops. Now, as ecological matters like environmental degradation and fatigue of the Green Revolution are popular topics, one could not miss the evidence how over the years the output of grain/rice had dropped due to intensification of agriculture and ecological degradation. Tractors and combines have replaced manual labour (no wonder the present generation does not need the traditional spade called *Kassi*; this traditional knowledge is nearly lost). Crop residue of rice is burnt, that of wheat it is preserved as fodder. Common property or grazing land for cattle, goats and sheep is absent. Animals are stall-fed. Bullock carts are not seen anymore. Buffaloes are the main source of milk. Milk and its derivatives are the staple diet in the Punjab.

We should also not forget the days of insurgency in the

Punjab which had joblessness as an important driver of the episode. The prosperity of Punjab in an era of joblessness, depletion of ground water and the trend in youth not finding employment or motivation in agriculture impacts on the psyche of the people. Now there is a need for an evergreen revolution and also preserving our biodiversity of crops and animals. These simple ecological, agricultural and employment matters now need much more attention. There is enough ecological challenge in the Punjab which demands formation of ETF for a beginning and deep changes in the political economy of wheat/rice multi-cropping cycle and measures to control depletion of ground water, waterlogging and salinity.

NOTES

1. See Rama Sharma and C.K.N. Thampi, "Environment and Hill Roads", *Oonchi Sadken,* Seminar Towards Better Road in Hill, New Delhi, Directorate General Border Roads, 8-9 October 1990, pp. 21-3.
2. *Climate Change 2007: Impact, Adaptation and Vulnerability,* Working Group II, IGPCC, 4 AR of 13 April 2007, p. 9.
3. "China Names Officials to Discuss Water Disputes", *Hindustan Times* (New Delhi), 12 June 2007.
4. *The Tribune* (New Delhi), 8 August 2005.
5. *National Forest Commission,* Government of India, 2006, Chapter 8, p. 136.
6. S.S. Negi, *Natural Resource Management in the Himalayas: Volume II, Silviculture of Himalayan Tress and Bamboos,* New Delhi: APH, 2003, pp. 202-3.
7. *Ibid.,* pp. 204-5.
8. *The Tribune* (New Delhi), 12 September 2007. The study rightfully suggests that the tree is recommended around waterlogged areas. This concept of vertical biological drainage is well known in waterlogged regions of canals in Rajasthan. I am also grateful to Colonel Chikara, the Commanding Officer in-charge of arboriculture in Faridkot Cantonment near Ferozepour in Punjab, for bringing to my notice the advantage of these species in chronic waterlogged areas due to extensive paddy cultivation such as in Faridkot, where one can see seepages crawling up the walls of buildings.
9. These insights are from a round table discussion (unpublished) held at the USI of India on 21 March 2005. I thank Professor Subhash

Chander and Shri D.K. Mehta, Commissioner of Indus, Ministry of Water Resources for their insights which have been included in parts in this chapter.

10. At Hussainiwala headworks I was briefed by the JCO in charge from the local Engineer Regiment that as the river criss-crosses before it enters India north of the place called Samike Tower, waste from a leather factory in Pakistan is being discharged which pollutes the water on the Indian side. I also saw water hyacinth. Both countries need to sort out this problem of intrusive species and pollution in an integrated manner.
11. The others being Bist doab (between Sutlej and Beas), Rechna doab (between Ravi and Chenab) and Chaj doab (between Chenab and Jhelum).

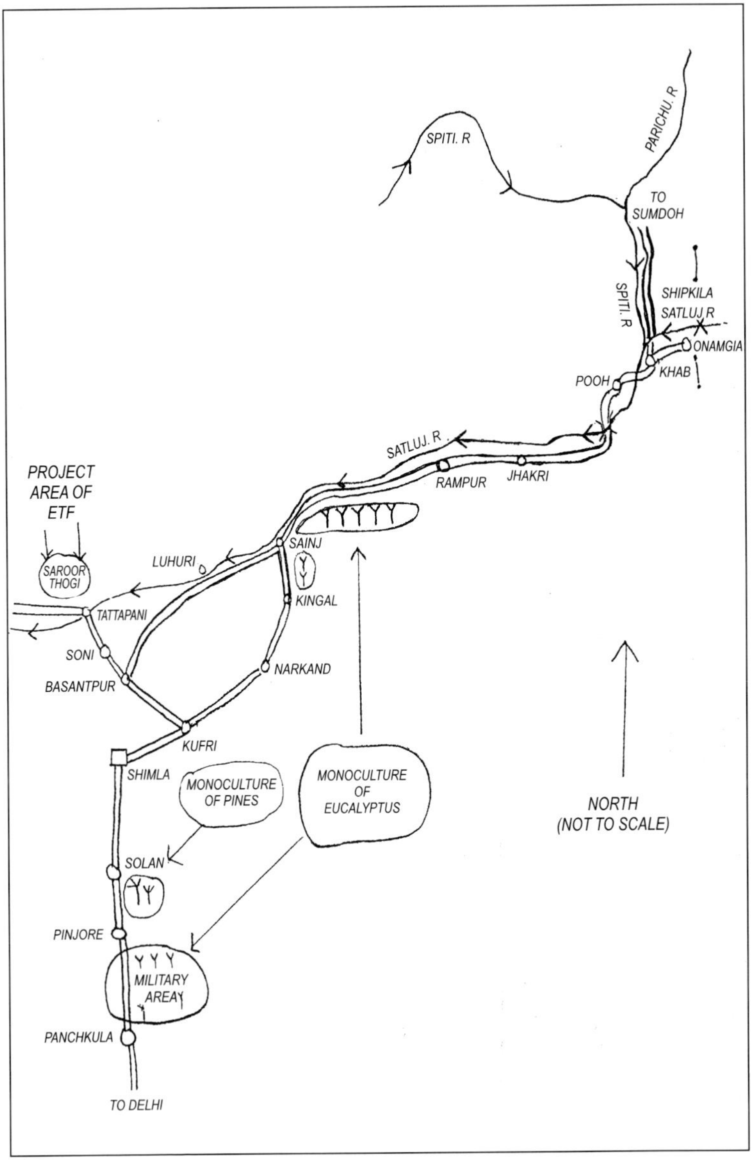

Satluj Watershed from Tattapani to Pooh.

Hill Feature that Needs to be Afforested by 133 ETF at Tattapani as on June 2007.

6

North-East India

In 2006, for the first time in its history the IDSA conducted a seminar outside Delhi by co-opting the North East Hill University and the North East Council. The seminar, held at Shillong, was titled "Peace and Development in the North-East".[1] Ecological problems were prominent in the discourse. Later, a field visit to the China-India border where the Siang (Brahmaputra) enters India in Arunachal Pradesh was made during the lean flow/pre-monsoon period in April 2007. The objective of the visit was to observe the ecology of the region and establish any ecological work that could be undertaken jointly with the Chinese near the border. Besides a study on the border region near the international border where the Siang enters India, the Department of Environmental Science at Tezpur University, Assam was also visited during the return journey en route to Guwahati. The invitation to visit the university was extended by Prof. K.K. Barua, Head of the Department of Environmental Science, as a follow-up to the IDSA seminar. Parts of upper Assam from Dibrugarh to Tezpur and Guwahati were also visited after over thirty years.[2] Professor Barua has rightly provided future developmental strategies based on a holistic approach consistent with environmental and social principles, which implies that the hills and adjoining plains must be taken as the macro-planning unit.[3] The environmental challenges and concerns have to be dovetailed with the trajectory of economic activities in the construction of infrastructure, agriculture and urbanisation. All have to be underscored with the social relationship the people have with Nature and the looming population growth.

Broad Overview of Ecology of Arunachal Pradesh[4]

How to treat, govern and integrate in the national mainstream the state of Arunachal Pradesh was guided by the seminal work of Verrier Elwin.[5] It goes to the credit of India that unlike China's case in Tibet, it allowed minorities, and especially the tribal people to retain their culture and identity. Special provisions of the Constitution such as the Sixth Schedule, Panchayati Raj Institutions and articles of the Constitution provide special privileges to the states of the North-East. While in one way this has led to the preservation of their identity, it has also led to compartmentalisation of people more and more on narrow tribal, linguistic and ethnic lines in the North-East. Population pressures such as immigration, rapid population growth and renewable resource scarcity such as land and competition for limited jobs have created a set of problems. Many states for a complex number of reasons have seen or are undergoing insurgency. But the case of Arunachal Pradesh is unique. The people here surprisingly speak fluent Hindi and have imbibed an Indian identity. They do not have an insular mentality.

But there have been problems of insensitivity to recognise the unique culture and people of the region. Indians from other parts of the country find it difficult to understand this unique culture and its links with Nature. The region is hilly. The people of hill regions of Uttarakhand and Himachal Pradesh probably connect better with the people of the North-East. But there is difference in racial characteristics, eating habits, language and religion.

In simple terms, there is a deficiency in our understanding of social anthropology. Nari Rustomji has eloquently expressed this problem in the region:

> The planning process concentrates attention on the intermediary stations—the achieving of targets of road construction, literacy and so on—without concern for the final end to which these intermediary stations are to lead. Bureaucrats and policy-makers have not been able to get over their prejudices against social anthropologists, who they look upon as a superfluous operator whose aim is

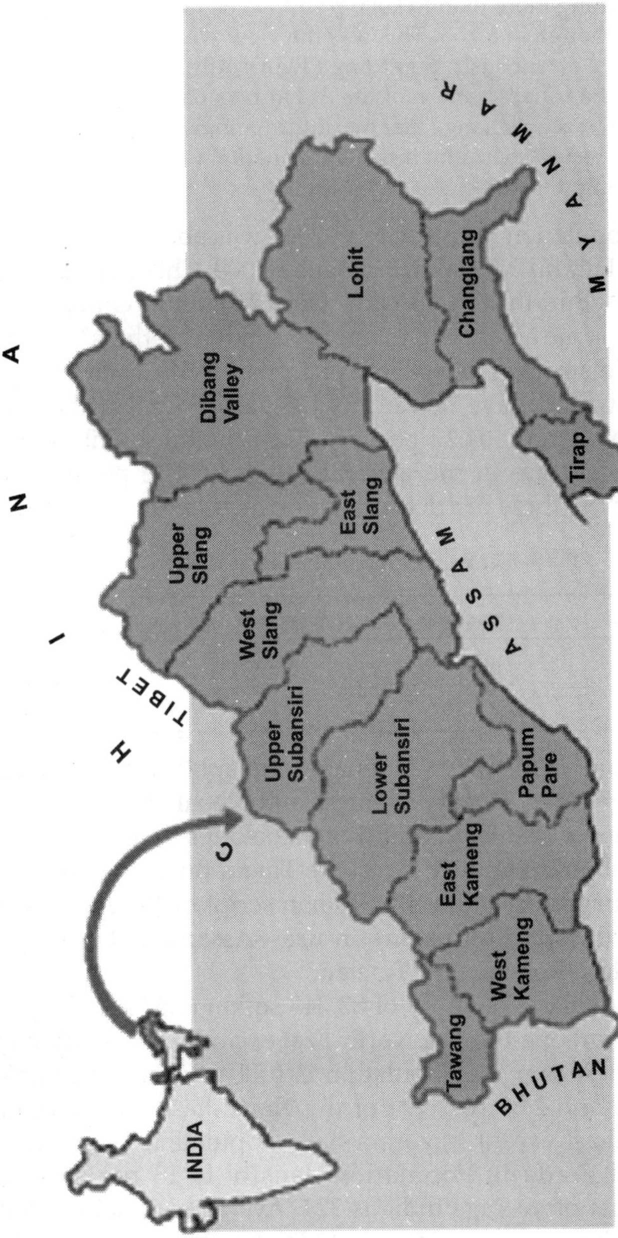

Location of Arunachal Pradesh

Source: Arunachal Pradesh Human Development Report 2005.

> nothing more than to keep primitive people segregated as though in a zoo. This was the view widely held, but quite erroneously, regarding Elwin's attitude to change in the tribal's pattern of life. What is not appreciated is that it is not change that the anthropologists oppose but the recklessness and lack of imagination with which it is brought about.[6]

The population of the state in 2001 was about one million (10 lakh—Hindus 3.79 lakh, Muslims 20,000, Christians 2 lakh, Sikhs 1865, Buddhists 1.43 lakh, Jains 216, and "Others" 3.3 lakh). It took me a field trip to understand that "others" means Donyi-Poloism. A good gazetteer update with each census probably would have made this job easier. Out of the one million population, 64.22 per cent are Scheduled Tribes and 35.78 per cent are in the general category. The population figures for the three districts of Siang are given in Table 6.1.

Table 6.1: Population of the Siang Region

District	*Population*	*Scheduled Tribes*	*General*
West Siang	1,0,3918	82%	18%
East Siang	87,397	70%	30%
Upper Siang	33, 363	78%	22%

As many as forty-two languages are spoken in the state. All the languages, except Assamese and Nepali, belong to the Tibeto-Chinese family. Khampti-Shan belongs to the Siamese-Chinese subgroup while the rest are Tibeto-Burman in origin. Most languages use either the Roman script or the Assamese script. Six different scripts are in use—Assamese, Devnagri, Hingna, Mon, Roman, and Tibetan.

The state has a territory of 83,743 sq km (2.55% of India's land area, and one-third of North-East excluding Sikkim). It is larger than Assam, its population is 0.11 per cent of India's population and 2.85 per cent of the North-East. All states of the North-East except Mizoram have population larger than Arunachal Pradesh. Population density is 13 per sq km, whereas that of average India is 324. Average annual rainfall is 350 cm with pre-monsoon period March/April and extremely wet season from June/July till September/October. Most of the terrain (96%) is hilly, with alpine, temperate and sub-tropical and semi-evergreen forests; 82 per cent of the region is covered with forests.

The state is endowed with a third of the 15,000 seed plants found in India. It has thousands of non-flowering plants, 500 exotic orchids and 450 medicinal plants, bamboos, canes, thatch grasses and wild bananas. In fauna, it has 100 species of mammals, 8 out of 16 species of primates found in India, bisons and mithuns, and a variety of species of birds (650), fishes (105) and amphibians (42).

***Mithuns* in Arunachal**

ndemic to North-East India's jungles, the *mithun (Bos frontalis)* is a rare bovine species. The ghest population of *mithuns* is in Arunachal (124,730 in 1998).

he animal is an integral part of the socio-economic and cultural life of the people. The wealth of a erson is often gauged by the number *of mithuns* he possesses. The *mithun* is regarded as a ymbol of prestige and was traditionally used as a medium of exchange, a means to settle disputes, nd as the bride price, *mithuns* determine social status. They also provide calories and protein, and e essential part of community feasts.

et, *mithuns* are reared in a free-range system. The owners leave the *mithuns* in the jungles to aze on natural fodder and they are occasionally given a dose of common salt. The *mithuns* owse over a considerable range in search of fodder and over two dozen species of trees, hrubs, tall grasses, and bamboos form their diet. To maintain these *mithuns*, the protection of e pristine forest is required, a task that is becoming increasingly difficult.

ource: Arunachal Pradesh Human Development Report, 2005.

Threats to Biodiversity

The state is under rapid transformation. Urbanisation, road and infrastructure construction, and illegal trade of timber, medicinal plants and orchids, and biopiracy have already taken their toll. The state's medicinal plants are endangered due to trade, habitat loss and natural calamities. Documentation is lacking. As has been seen, the 26 major tribes and 110 sub-tribes have script-less languages. For complete documentation of inherited ethnic knowledge of these people, a wholehearted joint effort by taxonomists, ethno-biologists and naturalists with locals is needed.[7]

Mishra and Datta point out that it is largely in the last decade that wildlife research and exploration began to gain momentum. They argue that a state with 80 per cent of the population being agriculturist is witnessing rapid socio-economic change. Its urban population has risen from near zero in 1961 to 25 per cent in 2001. There is a high degree of dependence on natural resources. Till 1996, the state was largely dependent on timber extraction for revenue, which was stopped after a ban by the Supreme Court. Paradoxically, the continued lack of livelihood opportunity has meant continued high dependence on natural resources. Hunting is no more sustainable as a part of the local culture and is leading to "empty forest syndrome", where the forest may appear intact but most of the wildlife population is heavily depleted or lost.[8] The authors are of the view that the underlying cause of uncertain status of biodiversity is non-involvement of the local communities in conservation though they own 62 per cent of forest land in the state. They are optimistic that in an era of specie extinction, a new specie of bird the Bugun Liocichla (Liocichla bugunorum)[9] offers a ray of hope in recording and preserving our biodiversity and community-based conservation.

Visit to the Sino-Indian Border in Siang Districts of Arunachal Pradesh: Ecological Aspects

Terrain and Climate

Map indicates the area of the North-East. Sketch 6.1 the route traversed from north to south from Dibrugarh. It needs to be noted that the north-to-south river valley systems of Arunachal Pradesh are not similar. Unlike the Tawang and Kameng region, this area is of relatively low mountains. The terrain rises through a series of foothills in the south to the Lesser Himalayas on the Tibet border. Massive hill features of over 10,000 feet dominate the interior valleys and still had snow cover on them. It was informed that as the monsoon broke all the snow would melt. The general height of the road axis/valleys is 600 to 1000 metres; the height of Tuting is 1050 metres and that of Gelling 1450 metres (95 degree easting, 29 degree northing) which is short of the Line of Actual Control (LAC) and the last village about 1500 metres from the LAC.

The climate in the foothills is sub-tropical. The temperature decreases rapidly with altitude. The average rainfall is 3500 mm a year. The area is abundantly forested from alpine in high regions to the subtropical and semi-evergreen. The area traversed along the road axis and the foot tracks is of the broad-leaved tropical jungles with thick wet temperate bamboo forests and wild bananas at places. Till Along the terrain and vegetation is like that in the Shivaliks. Ahead of Along, the rich biodiversity is amazing and unexpectedly devoid of popular trees such as deodars, pines and similar trees associated with my experience of the Himalayas in Jammu and Kashmir, Ladakh, Kumaon, Meghalaya and Kameng border regions. The type of forests with undergrowth were closer to the forests and jungles one studied in Burma. This contrast was indeed dramatic. Accounts of the 1962 Sino-Indian war in the region have incidents of withdrawing columns of the Indian Army dying of exhaustion when not lost in the thick jungles, but when negotiating peaks with early winter snow of November 1962. Unlike in popular imagination, Tibet is not all high-altitude plateau. The south-eastern parts closer to the LAC are similar to the terrain of Upper Siang district. In general the mountain system is fragile and the soil soft. No hard rocky outcrops as in the Western Himalayas were encountered. Geologists mention that in Siang rocks are carbonised or semi-carbonised. The forests here help in soil stabilisation, moisture retention for local rain, nutrient recycling and provide habitat for a rich biodiversity.

People of the Region

Arunachal Pradesh is home to 26 major tribes scattered in 3649 villages. The population of the state in the 2001 census was about one million with population of upper Siang over 33,000 (the ratio of Scheduled Tribes to general category is 78:22%). Broadly, the entire population in the Siang region (consisting of three districts of East, West and Upper Siang) could be divided in two groups based on the socio-political-religious affinities Adis and Buddhists.

Adis. The Adis (erstwhile barbarians Abors) populate the foothills till short of the LAC. Old maps still show the region as Abor hills. Their origin is from Tibet and according to the East Siang district web site, they are an Astro-Mongoloid group. They follow Donyi-Poloism. Their religious rituals coincide with phases of agriculture. They traditionally practise jhum agriculture, also termed "Adi-Arik". Settled agriculture, possible in low and flat river valley plains, is called "Asi-Arik". The term pani-kheti is more in use to refer to patches of settled agriculture. The people are independent-spirited, friendly and cheerful. Informally it was learnt that the quota for recruitment rallies conducted by the Indo-Tibetan Border Police (ITBP) was not fully subscribed. They are not keen to work as porters or as labour for road construction with the Border Road Organisation (BRO). Thus like in other regions of the Himalayas the BRO employs Bihari, Nepali and in this particular region tribal labour from Orissa. Ecological historian Ramachandra Guha in his work on colonialism and conflict in the Himalayan forests of Kumaon in the early twentieth century had shown how the locals avoided and disliked forced labour and work as porters. The hillmen, according to Guha, were unjustly commented upon by the officials. The hillman's aversion to work under compulsion had led to an undeserved reputation for indolence by the colonial rulers.[10] In an unpublished history of 4 Corps, titled "Born to Charge: History of 4 Corps" it has been mentioned that in 1973 Lt Gen I.S. Gill, PVSM, MC was critical of the attitude of officials at Along who he found outnumbered the locals during his visit. He famously mentioned that "I do not agree with many others who thought that the people were lazy. To me they just seemed to be contented". A spirited Regimental Officer of the Army Medical Corps with the BRO posted for the last two years at Moling said that though he found them about 1000 years in the past, he admired their attitude to life and happiness.

The Adis have the democratic tradition of village council or Kebang for collective decision-making. The forests are owned by the village council. Compensation has to be given for lifting and using of sand, boulders and similar material by the BRO to the individuals. The government does not own any forests (reserved or protected). Entry to the state by Indian nationals is governed by the Inner line Regulations[11] for which permission has to be obtained.

The people speak good Hindi. Modernisation is visible in the use of cell phones, dish TV and fashion-conscious youth of the towns on the main road axis. Modern passenger cars and motorcycles are also in good use.

The military officers at Along had mentioned that the local youth are against outsiders marrying the local girls, though one reception of a Bengali male government employee who had married a local colleague was being held at Along. One often hears the latest numbers from the Bombay film industry in their celebrations.

Film director and former Director of the Centre for Cultural Research and Documentation Moji Riba in an article in the Monsoon-Winter 2005 issue of the *IIC Journal* devoted to the North-East had referred to changes of the society. The old loose-knit functions were being now being organised on committee basis. Moji Riba's article also mentioned that Christianity was 10.3 per cent in 1991 and now it is 18 per cent. Scholar Talom Rukbo of Pasighat has suggested reviving and rejuvenating the traditional faith to stem Christianity, including establishment of prayer halls and giving forms to deities. Talom Rukbo observed a paradox of "more globalisation with more tribalisation". His theory holds a universal truth world wide, including in other parts of India, where society is also in the grip of identity crisis and leans back to the caste/tribe or clan.

Tuting: Tuting, a Buddhist region is full of prayer flags, chortens and mane walls. It is at an altitude of 1050 metres with a population of approximately 7000. It has a battalion location with other elements of paramilitary forces. It has a helipad and an advanced landing ground (ALG) fit to take AN-32 transport aircraft. It has a suspension bridge linking it with Jidu village to the east. A new road alignment by the Public Works Department (PWD) on the east bank of the river from Yingiong till Jidu with a motorable bridge at either end is being planned. At Tuting the most important set-up is the newly established measuring station of the Central Water Commission (CWC) established in 2006 to measure and record the flow of the Siang each day. It may be recalled that on 11 June 2000 flash floods caused heavy damage to property in the region. A flood had occurred two years earlier as well. Due to these flash floods India has a memorandum of understanding for sharing the river data of both the Sutlej and Siang with China, though no water sharing talks or agreements have taken place. The oldest member of CWC, one Shri Apang hailing from the village stated that while he understood the problem of glacier lake outburst floods (GLOF), the floods of 2000 were much stronger and even the ALG was under water. Later, while interacting with commanders and staff at higher formations it was told that even China (Tibet) suffered devastation of the 11 June 2000 event from which it is yet to fully recover.

Photograph 6.1 of the suspension bridge over the Siang indicates what traditional engineering feats are possible using cane and bamboo. Probably the day is not far when this knowledge may disappear.

Gelling: Gelling is the last village near the LAC. There is no motor road, though one is planned in the near future. The road head is at the village of Bona which is about 20 km north of Tuting. The march to Gelling is on a steep ascent and could take about three hours on a clear day. When my field visit was being planned, the General Officer Commanding of 2 Infantry Division was very keen to host a field study on the role of the military in ecological restoration. He noted that the study would also include Gelling, which was devastated by a giant mudslide on 13/14 April 2006 and where troops of the division had carried out rescue, relief and rehabilitation of the village. In the mudslide, for the first time in living memory Gelling village was partially washed away by a sudden cloudburst which left deep scars in the mountainside. Fortunately, there were no casualties as the school building which was in the path of the fury was unoccupied. Three persons of the Special Intelligence Bureau (SIB) had a miraculous escape as their hut was saved the fury, though huge boulders had flown down on either side with the mudslides.

A similar cloudburst had also taken place over Tibet (China) across the international border as was also visible from view point 2073.

The village is in the process of being relocated on a ridge nearby with the name of Narboling (new village). A 50 kW micro-hydro project is being set up nearby for which lines are yet to be laid. Some houses have solar-powered batteries (Tata Deep) recently supplied to the civilians and the ITBP.

Influence of Mahayana Buddhism: The Khambas and Membas of Gelling and Tuting are Buddhists. The ubiquitous lama prayer flags, *chortens* and *manes* are indications of their faith. Shri Dorji Sangal, the chowkidar at the inspection bungalow Gelling mentioned that they were Membas with affiliation to Buddhism as in Bhutan. According to information with the ITBP, in the academic year 2007, about 15 children from Gelling had left for Tibetan boarding schools affiliated to the Dalai Lama all over India. This is normal practice. Also men from the local villages such as Bishing are serving as soldiers of the Indian Army. As far as cross-border contacts are concerned in the general region there are three old ladies hailing from villages across the border who were married before 1962. The war put an end to the contacts with Pemako and Chimdru regions. Overall, the relation of ITBP with the locals is warm. With lure of urbanisation it was also learned that some soldiers serving in the Indian Army are tending to settle down outside the state such as in Dehradun where affordable housing societies are coming up. Such sociological changes are inevitable.

Visit to the LAC View Point 2073 to Observe the Siang

With full support and briefing provided by ITBP under the able leadership of Sub Inspector J.C. Jishtu of the Gelling post, a patrol under Havildar Govardhan of ITBP with another constable of ITBP and Naik Sardeep Rautela of 9 Kumaon as escort left Gelling at 0630 hours and were able to reach the only view point (short of Point 2073) from where Tibet (China) is visible, including the Siang. The LAC was about 200 metres away on a steep fall. Negotiating the area other than over beaten tracks along spurs requires mountaineering gear and skills. The path was also infested with leaches. No ancient trade route for man pack or animal pack tracks exists nearby. Sketch 6.2 shows the route with LAC and Photograph 6.2 shows the Siang river before it enters India. The LAC does not follow any watershed principle, as was imagined, as the features criss-cross. Probably, on small-scale maps they provide a conceptual arrangement to divide an area. Terrain in Tibet was like own side. Scars of mudslides due to cloudbursts were also observed on the hill slopes which had become bald with scars. Village Shirang in Tibet, approximately 5 km away, was also visible. Unlike the Indian side the huts were more aligned and regimented. The features of Gwala Peri and Namche Barwa where the Siang takes a U-bend were not visible, though from the map they were about 100 km to the north by north-east (about 10 degrees).[12] From literature survey as also from the internet it had been gathered that as the Brahmaputra enters India there is a great fall. This is not true. The U-bend and the region of the legendary waterfall discovered in 1999 is about 100 km away. The flow of the Siang in Tibet was along the low valleys as it entered India.

Lifestyle: The absence of pack animals such as ponies or donkeys or draught animals was conspicuous. Even in settled agriculture human power and energy was being used. The people here do not relish milk. Mithuns or Bos frontalis are socio-economic status symbols and like investments to be consumed on festivals. Wealth is measured by mithuns (see page 87). A very shy animal, belying its look. Mithuns are endemic to the region and are reared in free-range system, which is now under pressure due to shrinking and non-availability of pristine forests. The people are also hunter-gatherers, with excellent skills at shooting and trapping. If imparted proper training, experienced military officers considered them ideal guerrilla fighters in this type of terrain. They are non-vegetarians and eat herbs, leaves, hand-milled cereals, meat, fish, eggs, bamboo shoots, and green leafy vegetables.

Analysis and Policy Relevance

Inner Line Restrictions and Ecology

Perhaps the region of Siang districts does not suffer from severe environmental degradation as in other parts of India. The biodiversity is phenomenal. The continuation of the Inner Line permit possibly has helped in checking of illegal migrants and overpopulation. Habitat loss, road construction and urbanisation are already recognised as threats to biodiversity. Rare medicinal plants are also endangered. Thus opening up the line may be a recipe for ecological disaster for this "last bastion of diversity, and an exceptional heritage". Sanjib Baruah in his *Post Frontier Blues* holds the view that the Inner Line of Arunachal Pradesh, Mizoram and Nagaland has been misused. He cites the famous case of Bengali migrant Jamir Ali working as a sharecropper in Dikang Valley near Itanagar.[13] While his observation is relevant, the terrain in Siang was probably different. This difference in terrain is the likely reason why Apatanis, who live in that region have adopted settled cultivation. After India declared its Look East policy in the 1990s, entry restrictions which then applied to Assam, Meghalaya and Tripura were lifted.[14] This is definitely a new research agenda, but for purely ecological reasons the restrictions at least in Arunachal Pradesh need to be continued.[15]

Forests

According to one mainstream opinion, slash or burn or swidden (jhum) is a highly environmentally destructive activity. This has happened as a result of shortening of the cycle from ten to fifteen years to about five years due to population pressures, no less than those illegally from Bangladesh. Planting of experimental tea has been suggested.

R. Manhas *et al.* (from the Forest Research Institute and Forest Survey of India) have shown that in the North-East jhum (which is 85% of total cultivation) is the only reason for deforestation. The decrease in forest cover in the North-East due to jhum is 23 per cent during 1984-1994 (Manipur 14.1%, Assam 12.9%, Arunachal Pradesh 11.2%, Nagaland 16.7%, Mizoram 26.9% and Meghalaya 17.5%).[16]

So what needs to be done? P.S. Ramakrishnan recommends that traditional ecological knowledge (TEK) has a strong human element attached to it and jhum needs to be built up on TEK or redeveloped rather than providing an alternative to jhuming.[17] It is hoped that greater participation by local communities to understand the switch over is provided for a smoother transition.

Why has not a Chipko movement or its equivalent taken place in the North-East? The Chipko movement was started by the women of Garhwal Himalayas who were protesting against the felling of trees by the contractors. In one way the Supreme Court ban on logging has put an end to the threat to the forests. But it will be unfair not to recognise the preservation of forests by the people of Arunachal Pradesh. The anthropologist J.J. Roy Burman has pointed out that Arunachal Pradesh, with 64 per cent forest cover has only 18.86 per cent of it under reserve category, which means that a great deal of the people's participation has gone into the upkeep of the state's forests.[18] Tiplut Nonbri, citing the case of Meghalaya, mentions that the ban has also affected the people's livelihood based on non-timber forest products (NTFP) and has led to pauperisation.[19] Ecologically harmful charcoal production by cutting trees and stems is another way the forest dwellers in Meghalaya have resorted to for survival.[20]

There is a need to survey, study and audit the decadal impact due to the Supreme Court ban which began in December 1996. Unfortunately, we all seem to agree in the deliberations that in spite of the ban illegal logging takes place. This illegal logging needs to be clarified. Surely, all the harm done is not due to charcoal production. The delivery of governance may be at fault. Experts were queried on the process to establish forest degradation by remote sensing as it was assumed by lay persons that it could provide useful indications. But things are not so simple.

Difficulty with this approach (remote sensing) is that after illegal removal the area gets green cover very quickly because of suitable climate for bamboo growth. Meaning thereby that structure of forest is changing without affecting much the most talked about parameter—forest cover. If you want the holistic view then you have to conduct what is known as forest inventory in the concerned area. This work is being carried out by Forest Survey of India and published in State Forest Report-2003 and being updated in forthcoming SFR-2005. This is, of course, through sampling providing the information of change in wood volume rather than mapping the area.[21]

Perhaps identification, recording and survey of the data on deforestation by jhum separately and illegal logging is an emerging challenge for administrators in the region. But people's participation may be the ultimate solution.

Jhuming

With sparse population, the jhuming cycle is over ten to fifteen years or more. Ecological degradation as is happening in other parts of the North-East is not as acute (as yet). However, military officers who have flown in helicopters over the area and have seen hills not visible from the road fear that severe ecological degradation may soon set in due to massive balding of features due to jhuming. It was found that where possible settled agriculture or *pani kheti* was being done. But such flat patches are extremely limited in at least the Siang region. However, to expect all to convert to settled agriculture is not to understand the socio-psychological roots. The problem is that jhum—as a major cause of concern in receding forest cover—is being transformed into settled agriculture or prevented through legislation. As Mihin Dollo and others point out, what is not understood holistically is people's perceptions and customary laws including land tenure system.[22]

It was very difficult to establish the areas in various phases of jhum like recently burned, current jhum ready for harvesting, recovery in five, ten or more years, and so on. Probably this information is with the village Kebangs. Scholars point out that in Arunachal Pradesh jhum is 1.10 lakh hectares of land (1.7% of geographic area) and is much less than the area destroyed by loggers.[23] About 35 crops are cultivated in a jhum cultivation system which are traditional cultivars that the local people have been conserving from time immemorial.[24] It has been pointed out that jhum cultivation seems to better conserve the diversity of crops compared to modern agro-forestry. There is thus a need to carry out scenario planning based on time-series data and confirm if, as in other parts of India, would jhuming here lead to severe ecological degradation. The local community and Kebangs must be involved in this study together with the district administration who have the authority and the wherewithal to establish a scientific basis. If it is found that the process is sustainable, there is no need for urban planners to decry the process and use a one-size-fits-all template and force an unimplementable solution down their throats. It needs to be remembered that jhuming is all organic, it needs no energy inputs like fertilisers or pesticides or draught power. Due to steep slopes on mostly massive features settled agriculture appears to be a formidable task. One also needs to remember that for settled agriculture deforestation takes place. P.S. Ramakrishnan from the School of Environmental Sciences, Jawaharlal Nehru University, New Delhi in his research has shown that farmers have rejected replacing shifting agriculture by sedentary terrace farming as it demands high energy inputs like fertilisers and pesticides. He shows that the reason for the rejection is that as soil cover is thin and infertile, the nutrient losses from this system are heavy, and more and more fertilisers are required to sustain sedentary practices.[25] In a lecture delivered at the G.B. Pant University of Agriculture and Technology he mentioned that external pressures arising from governmental policies and market pressures (both national and/or international) are the key drivers of large-scale land degradation.[26] He showed that while textbook-based "formal knowledge" has its value, the rich traditional ecological knowledge derived through an experimental process and available with the local communities forms a powerful connecting link between ecological and social systems. In this light he champions the redevelopment of jhum through an "incremental pathway" through community participation.

Jhuming is no easy job and appears to be harder than settled agriculture. Most of the terrain has tough gradients with thick forests. Unlike the Kangra region or Kumaon (from where probably the top-down scientific view of improving agricultural practices originates) the hills are not gently sloping where terraced fields can be developed.

The new challenge is that with modernisation of the village lifestyle, people are migrating to small townships. Also education and training facilitating off-farm employment have led to the reduction of active human power in the rural areas for farming. Eventually, some of the younger generation are completely deprived of the knowledge about "jhuming" as such. So, it may be presumed that shifting cultivation would cease automatically with the demise of the older generation.[27]

Road Construction and Maintenance

Accelerated road building is in progress wherein more north-south roads will be developed and east-west cross-valley links established. As these are not rush jobs forced by warlike conditions, a proper ecological assessment would need to be done using historical data, new technology and innovation so that road building is not a cause of landslide, and soil erosion later. Rushing through to complete jobs may achieve short-term targets of road construction, but may lead to disruption in the long term if all holistic ecological factors are not taken into account. This would lead to disruption in communication in the long run. Thus it is both in the interest of civil and military that utmost care is taken on ecological matters. It is obvious that the costs may go up, but by avoiding future blocks the recurring operating and maintenance costs may come down. BRO with its magnificent performance and good practices is surely tackling this challenge and the Public Works Department also needs to be co-opted.

The history of road building in India shows that as roads develop, massive logging and deforestation takes place by vested business interests. In central India, not only the Naxals but some sections of the people fear that roads may lead to the end of the forest dwellers. This should not be allowed to happen here. Notwithstanding the decade-old Supreme Court ban on felling of trees in the North-East, innovative methods can be adopted to bypass the law. In the chapter on sustainable development the *Arunachal Pradesh Human Development Report 2005* notes:

> Road networks have linked the plains with the hills, and opened up hitherto impenetrable regions. In the fragile and relatively young geological system of the Eastern Himalayas, these have left scars on the countryside; the roads will take many years to stabilise, and the scars even more time to heal.[28]

Ecology near LAC

There appears no manmade ecological degradation near the LAC. Cloudbursts are indeed acts of Nature and care may be needed to site buildings safe from mudslides. The ecological challenge in India and Tibet is preserving the ecology as road communications are built up.

The Brahmaputra

Maps can be deceptive. The Brahmaputra has many claims to its origin. Within India, starting east to west the branches flowing in from the north are the Lohit, Dibang or Sikang, Siang, Subansiri and Kameng. The Dihang, Dibang and Lohit provide 50 per cent of the average flow. Subansiri with another 10 per cent. The longest tributary is Yarlung Zangpo or Tsangpo as it leaves on its eastward journey from Mount Kailash across southern Tibet. In Tibet the prominent glacier-fed tributaries are Raga Tsangpo, Nien-chu-ho, La-sa-ho (one account claims that it is three kilometres broad), Yarlungchu and Niyongpo. It thereafter tapers down and skirts between Gyala Peri (7150 m) and Namche Barwa (7756 m) and takes a U-turn as it cascades down the Tibetan plateau to lower heights and enters India north of Gelling. In Arunachal Pradesh itself, the Siang receives nine tributaries in its 200 km journey.

While negotiating the river at ferry north of Dibrugarh (the water of Siang, Dibang and Lohit) in April, it was the lean period with depth of 3 feet just about adequate for a 12-ton light ferry. The ferry operator mentioned that the lean period is from December till March. Over the last fifteen years, he observed, the river has broadened and eats into the bank (bank erosion). With broadening, its depth has also reduced. It may be recalled that Dibrugarh is being swamped slowly and in the earthquake of 15 August 1950, Sadia town was washed away in landslips that blocked the Dibang which later burst. The impact of river diversion on restricting ferry operations in the lean period is not well understood. In river terrain as in Assam or Bangladesh this aspect is vital. Scholars dealing with sharing of river waters with Bangladesh need to understand the fear lower riparian harbours on this account. Another great opportunity in the era of global warming is to cut road transport and rely on inland waterway transport in a big way.

The difficulty of terrain and absence of roads does not lend itself to the idea that India and China could jointly harness the immense hydroelectric potential at the U-bend. Probably, the road network in Tibet may be better developed to reach that site. If the Chinese have to generate hydroelectricity (other than micro-projects which are the norm), they are within their rights to build dams on the Yarlung Zangpo or Tsangpo. The flow should not be at the cost of our share during the lean period. However, the greatest public fear is the diversion of the Brahmaputra by China.[29]

The Brahmaputra has not been studied as much as the Ganga. We know from the work of Sunil K. Singh *et al.* that the Eastern Syntaxis basin of the Brahmaputra is one of the most intensely chemically eroding regions of the globe; and the runoff and physical erosion are the controlling factors of chemical erosion in the eastern Himalaya.[30] The contribution of the north and south bank distributaries of the Brahmaputra to erosion and siltation is also significant. The combined effect of soil erosion and silt deposition would create new soil profiles. Measures need to be initiated when the soil samples could be tested and the right micro-nutrients provided and proper seeds sown. This would require infrastructure and communications. As we have to live with nature it is essential that we gear up to this emerging problem in a scientific manner and prepare to deliver doable and workable solutions to the farmers.

Need for Nurturing of Mahayana Buddhism in India

It is important to understand the strong influence of Buddhism near the LAC. People here are highly nationalistic and content. They have faith in the educational infrastructure set up by the Tibetans in India. They also serve in the Indian Army in Vikas battalions and Special Frontier Force. The policy so far to provide support and shelter to Tibetans in exile also indirectly helps our people having faith in various shades of Tibetan Buddhism and must be nurtured.[31]

Need for Gazetteers

Though the internet does have some information, there is a need to have comprehensive gazetteers of the districts within the state covering all aspects of the district. This will also be a good guide to central government officials and the military establishment to know the area and people well, as they are frequently turned over. This document will also come handy for scholars and travellers.

Institutionalisation of the Study of Local Culture by Military Officers and Government Officials Serving in the Region

The inspiration for this policy suggestion has been the Medical Officer posted with the BRO. It is very rare that officials of all-India service get a chance to serve in the region. But those who serve must be made to learn the culture of the region. This is being done in the normal routine, but it is more a function of individuals' preferences. What the military needs to do is beyond the so-called Sadbhavana model. They also need to learn the local culture and study the cultural anthropology in the situation that the locals face. Though the British had their colonial interests to serve, they cannot be faulted on the level of focused study of the people, flora and fauna of India. We need to imbibe this urge to excel in our officers serving in the region. It is time for mainstream India to study and learn best practices from ecological knowledge and social anthropology.

Teeth to Tail Ratio

Though not a focus of the field trip, one could not ignore that one rifle company needs to be deployed for line of communication duties catering for billeting, food and other related administrative arrangement in daily maintenance of troops. This information may be of some help to defence economists.

Environmental Issues in Some Parts of North-East India

Economic Roots of Insurgency

Renewable resources like timber and opium are resources that also feed this underground economy. Though literature on this subject exists on other regions of the world, sufficient empirical analysis or theoretical concepts have still not been developed for the states of India in this region by our own efforts. Sanjib Baruah in *Durable Disorder*[32] has alluded to the work of economist Paul Collier.[33] According to Collier, it is not poverty that breeds armed civil conflict but certain economic conditions which are conducive to mobilising revenue by armed insurgent groups. Primary commodities like tea, timber and coal are highly lootable and their production centres are located in conflict zones. According to Sanjib Baruah, the Collier thesis is useful in explaining the resilience of North-East insurgencies as these lootable commodities are conducive to illegal taxes.

In 1999 Paul Collier with colleague Anke Hoeffler studied the economics of conflict and violence. This "Collier-Hoeffler" (CH) model confirmed the link between poverty and conflict. One controversial finding was the greed versus grievance debate which posited that though initially grievance may be the main cause of insurgency, it transforms into a pursuit of greed. The growing literature by economists on grievance turning into greed indicates this trend. In other words, the ideology of the insurgency gets marginalised and greed driven by lootable natural resources is sufficient incentive for sustained criminalisation of the insurgency. The body of knowledge that links environmental factors (natural resources) with violent conflict is indeed multidisciplinary, spanning topics such as the environment and the political economy of insurgency.

Linking Ecological Episodes With Insurgency and Learning from the Past

Bamboo flowering or mautam in the 1960s was the trigger event that led to famine and insurgency in Mizoram. The cycle is in the process of revisiting the North-East. The Muli bamboo (Melocanna baccifera) is associated with famine and ecological disasters. That gregarious flowering occurs has been reported from 2004. Bamboo flowering brings famine as the gregarious flowering produces large quantities of seed that, in turn, causes a sudden population explosion in rats. When the quantity of seeds diminishes due to germination, the rodents head towards farmlands, granaries, godowns and households causing widespread loss of crops and spread of disease.[34] It has been mentioned that adequate precautions by way of storage of grains using modern technology have been taken. However, as Amartya Sen referring to the Irish and Bengal famines in the context of the memory of injustice and bitterness points out, "The memory of destitution and devastation tends to linger on, and can be invoked and utilised to generate rebellion and violence."[35] We need to be conscious of this episode and take all the precautionary principles and an ecologically sound way. The bamboo phenomenon shows that we have been able to identify one of the causes of insurgency and likewise social scientists need to be proactive in identifying other causes and take proactive preventive measures.

Urbanisation

Mizoram is the most urbanised state. Most of the north-eastern states are in the hills and thus have much in common with other hill stations in the Himalayas, Nilgiris or the Western Ghats. The urbanisation trend is world wide. What can we learn from the experience of urbanisation of cities located in the hill stations elsewhere in India such as Nainital, Mussoorie, Shimla, Darjeeling, Shillong or Udhagamandalam (Ooty)? A concrete jungle has emerged on steep gradients. Natural springs have been replaced with leaking sewage pipes on hill slopes that have been ruthlessly dug. The roots of trees choke as a result of concrete and garbage piles up on slopes which may be out of sight. Traffic jams and urban pollution as a result with ubiquitous cars are the norm and the lure of motor transport has made the tough hill folk reluctant walkers. We can remove the ill effects of rapid urbanisation by learning from the rapid growth of hill towns. There are some classic examples of theories of urban growth. One popular example is the comparison of Los Angeles and Chicago. The former grew haphazardly, the latter to a plan.[36] In similar fashion, the ills of rapid urbanisation in the hills of India can be theorised and future development based on revised models, taking into account practical and grassroots lessons, including measures to deal with increasing urban poverty. Also, there is an appreciable growth of the construction sector in the North-East.[37] The need is to take preventive measures in construction to minimise the damage as a result of earthquakes that may strike the region. Like traditional water harvesting, municipal laws must be put in place to take care of the earthquakes. The 8 October 2005 earthquake in Jammu and Kashmir, which included cities in Pakistan-Occupied Kashmir such as Muzaffarabad, showed that traditional structures suffered the least. Haphazard and quick-fix type of work was the worst affected.

The Impact of Dams

One central issue which needs to be addressed is where are the economic and environmental concerns going to clash. One clear indication is the complex response to the idea of big dams. We know that Arunachal Pradesh has blue gold to be used for generation of power of a potential of about 50,000 megawatts.

The Government of Arunachal Pradesh and the National Hydro Power Corporation, National Thermal Power Corporation and NEEPCO have signed a memorandum of understanding on 21 September, 2006 for developing about 15,000 MW of hydroelectricity. The major rivers on which these projects would be constructed are the Siang, Dibang, Subansiri, Lohit, Kameng and Tawanchu.[38] Concerns on the seismic, social and ecological aspects have been articulated in many forums.[39] Some organisations have been opposing mega dams since the Brahmaputra Board first conceived the Siang project in 1984. The Centre for Science and Environment in its flagship journal has a cover story on the acute stresses that the Tipaimukh dam would have in Manipur and how the civil society has formed the Action Committee against Tipaimukh Project (ACTIP).[40]

On the other hand, a recent World Bank study has emphasised the need for India to build dams. *India Water Economy: Bracing for a Turbulent Future* (2006),[41] which is based on twelve papers written by Indian authors, mentions that dams in the Himalayas are the most socially and environmentally benign in the world.

While discussing this topic, it may not be possible to take a "position" on dams: but it is clear that opinions are going to be split on the issue not unlike what we saw over the Narmada in central India. As the *Arunachal Pradesh Human Development Report 2005* has pointed out, "a state with potential of supplying one-third of total hydroelectricity to the country is buying power, and 46 per cent by diesel generated sets. The total installed capacity is just 58.95 MW". Purely from the need for generation of electricity like the Bhutan model it makes good economic sense to build dams. But the perspective of human, ecological and social impact on the project-affected people and submergence of traditional modes of collective agriculture poses the potential for social turmoil. Unlike China, which displaced more than a million people to build the Three Gorges dam, democratic India should not follow a ruthless path for what the urban planners and economists see as a common and larger good. Probably, micro-projects and run-of-the-river schemes provide suitable alternatives.

Mining

Unplanned and at places illegal mining of coal as in Meghalaya has led to pollution and loss of biodiversity.[42] Limestone quarrying in the caves of Meghalaya also poses serious ecological risks.[43] Plans to mine uranium reserves to sustain nuclear energy are also meeting resistance of local groups in Meghalaya. Thus, nearly all mineral extraction processes will come under increasing public and media scrutiny. A regeneration and revival ecological plan of the surgery performed on the land must be made mandatory.

Smuggling and Theft of Biodiversity

The North-East is one of the richest regions in biodiversity. It is well known that habitat loss is the biggest culprit for the loss of biodiversity. One threat that we need to guard against is cross-border poaching, smuggling and theft of genetic material for external commercial utilisation and safeguarding the patenting of processes and products.[44]

Greenhouse Gas Inventory from Paddy Fields

In the early 1990s some Western non-governmental organisations (NGOs) incorrectly calculated methane emissions from Indian cattle and paddy fields. The study, which placed the major share of global warming on Indian methane, was challenged by the government and Indian NGOs. This timely action forced the United Nations to accept the Indian calculation and data. Tezpur University is generating data specific to the North-East. Armed with these data, we will be able to negotiate better in international forums and also take measures to mitigate the impact of greenhouse gases.

Look East Policy

The Look East policy has three components—sea-borne trade and commerce, the medium of air travel for business and tourism, and the improvement of land communications from the North-East of India to the East. The third land component is vital to pursue a multi-pronged strategy.

Border trade is the starting block. The initiative to get the Nathu La trade route reopened was taken by the government of Sikkim.[45] In similar light there is immense potential for border states such as Mizoram, Manipur and Nagaland to further improve on the trade. To get the project moving, infrastructure like roads and storehouses need to be built. Interestingly, the Indian security establishment does not treat roads as a "threat" or an approach for an adversary to use for offensive operations. The transportation corridors, including reopening of Ledo Road, do not have any security consideration in the old mould. We need to compare the regions of Myanmar and Yunnan as the future of regionalism. The Look East policy thus must have its roots in the region.

Regionalism with trade links is growing. There is the concept of the two Punjabs between India and Pakistan. In similar manner we need to derive mutual benefit by encouraging regional and border trade. Initiatives like Kunming, BIMSTEC, and so on need to be sustained or revived where the enthusiasm may have waned.

The time is not far when India may get access to Chittagong port to move goods to the North-East. Good relations with Bangladesh are the key. The future of surface communications, energy infrastructure and inland water transport pathways is bright and all countries in the region would benefit in the long run through cooperation. Economic logic is likely to overcome any misgivings the countries may have on account of historical baggage.

Some Local issues of Border Trade

The Chief Minister of Mizoram was not happy with the present state of affairs in border trade, as the local economy was not in the process.[46] Smuggled goods do not allow the local economy to prosper. This has to be seen in the Look East policy and policy planners and those responsible for trade need to encourage the growth of the local economy. Another important issue in border trade is not allowing smuggling of acetic anhydride, a chemical essential for making fine-grade heroin in Mizoram and other states bordering Myanmar.[47] To sustain peace this link has to be stopped and the nexus that operates it needs to be exposed and punished. Perhaps a people's movement to stop this trade may emerge.

Indo-Tibetan Border Trade

Another low-volume trade that was impacted was in the trans-Himalayan region on the Bhutias after the 1962 border war. Though Nathu La has since been opened up for trade, it needs to be remembered that the nomads were also dependent on trade on either side. The chief economic wealth of Tibet lies in its nomad trade and cattle breeding. The nomad trade is in two forms. One is animal products like sheep skin, meat, milk and butter. Another is the use of pack animals such as yaks, dzos (cross breeds) and goats and sheep for trade. The Russian Tibetanist Roerich has mentioned that depriving Tibet of its cattle breeding region would lead to starvation in the Tibetan region.[48]

People's Attitude to Work

An important sociological aspect which needs to be deliberated upon is the attitude to work of the people in a particular region and their degree of satisfaction and aspirations. One often compares the examples of the industrious Sikh farmers turning the terai in the Himalayan foothills (now in Uttarakhand) into another Punjab by converting a harsh malarial terrain of sarkanda grass into the most productive agricultural region. Why is it that the hill people of the Kumaon and Garhwal Himalayas could not take advantage of this land on their own? How is that successful truckers' business and other business enterprises, that important provision stores and the like have been established by enterprising Sikhs? One reason is the gift of the Punjabi business acumen and entrepreneurship, as has been recorded in Prakash Tandon's excellent trilogy *Punjabi Saga*.[49] It is also pointed out by some that the hill people's lack of enterprise is linked to an attitude of fatalism, preferring to leave the land fallow and survive as subsistence farmers than undertake the enterprise of double or triple cropping to generate a surplus.[50]

During a seminar on Himalayan ecology at the Tata Energy Research Institute (since renamed as The Energy Research Institute) in 2001 where grassroots environmentalists such as Chandgi Prasad Bhatt also participated, this issue was deliberated upon. It was argued that one reason why ecological degradation by way of deforestation is in check is this very "want limitation" philosophy of the hill folk. They seem to be satisfied with minimum necessities. Yet, talking to some Manipuris we are told that this stereotypical "lazy" label needs to be challenged when one compares the feats of the insurgents from the region (which surely is sustained hard work).

Drawing parallels with the want limitation attitude of the people of the North-East and a sample of those from Uttarakhand hills one may need to understand the socio-cultural attitude. While at no stage it is implied that we "worship poverty", as economist Meghnad Desai avers in a television interview, we certainly need to deliberate on this fascinating sociological comparison. It is no surprise that there is no caste system in the region and most of the business or Vaishya space has been occupied by the Marwari community who have an inherent flair for trade.

Verrier Elwin too had alluded to this philosophy in his work when he cautioned that we need to be very careful in not upsetting the way the people of the North-East treat Nature.[51] Probably, our management and business models derived from our experiences in other parts of commercial India may not be suitable in the region if a one-size-fits-all model is attempted. Special status to the states in the region may also imply special understanding of the attitude of the "economic" person. We should also not forget that though Punjab, Haryana and western Uttar Pradesh once flourished under the Green Revolution, now the soil is over-chemicalised, the groundwater has been depleted and at places mined. Waterlogging and salinity are taking their toll. As a result, farmer suicides in the Punjab are rising. According to the agricultural scientist M.S. Swaminathan, there is a need to have an Evergreen Revolution in the regions not visited by the earlier Green Revolution. East India has sufficient groundwater resources which can help farmers to grow better crops with improved yield and thus help in achieving food security. But we also should be alert to a high degree of arsenic in the groundwater in the region. Perhaps the failure of the monsoon in 2006 has upset the Sali (kharif) crop of paddy in Assam. The infrastructure to use groundwater is poorly developed. This drought including the one in 2009 as the book goes to press thus may be a trigger event in taking a holistic view of irrigation in the plains.

Captains of industry, commerce and business are now taking a keen interest in agriculture. They may often lecture from success stories from other parts of India. The people of North-East India have a unique human-Nature relationship. While more productivity, double/triple cropping, not leaving land fallow are observations that satisfy a reductionist view, it is not sufficient to grasp the nuanced relationship of want limitation. The best long-term policy may be the evolution and improvement of eco-friendly and sustainable agricultural practices from within the region rather than transplanting models from other parts of India.

Travel Through Upper Assam After Three Decades: A Time-series Analysis

A total distance of about over 500 km was traversed from Likabali to Tezpur-Guwahati. The journey was through the districts of Dhemaji, Lakhimpur, Tezpur (Sonitpur), Darang, Mangaldoi and Guwahati. The towns of Tezpur and Mangaldoi were being visited after thirty-five years. As it was a counterinsurgency area, the army division insisted I do not venture on my own and preferred that I travel by hired transport organised by them. Thus, in a way it is difficult for an Indian citizen to back-pack and travel spontaneously in that region. It is to be hoped that when things improve this region gets its deserved share of travellers, giving a boost to the economy.

The driver of the hired transport provided by the army for the move was a retired Subedar hailing from Tezpur. He mentioned that there is no extortion and the ex-servicemen are not touched. He also mentioned that over the last three decades the population of ex-servicemen has increased and is better represented than in earlier times. This is a welcome development.

Since the last thirty-five years there has been a sea-change. The roads and bridges have improved. The BRO is double-laning the national highway. Nondescript towns like Tezpur have a smart look. The sleepy planters' town of Mangaldoi has changed and grown rapidly and one could no longer identify old landmarks.

Therè is a greater preponderance of migrants such as Bangladeshi Muslims than in the past. Only at Mangaldoi and a few other places the Assamese people could be seen in their traditional dresses. However, one has to live with this reality and adjust accordingly. Over centuries outside labour has poured into the Assam plains. Unlike Nagaland, Mizoram or Arunachal Pradesh there is no restriction of an Inner Line in the state. The identity crisis and the grievance about lack of job opportunities among the Ahoms is understandable. Ahom literature prides itself as not being subjugated by the Mughals. Even the history of Arunachal Pradesh has been reconstructed with the *Buranjis* (chronicles) of the Ahoms. Till the defeat at the hands of the Burmese they ruled the area for six hundred years, which included the hill regions. Prior to Ahoms the Bodos and Dimasas also share a proud heritage of their rule.

Overall, the sense or level of poverty was not very visible. Probably, this was because of driving along a highway and not visiting interior areas.

The beauty of the area is striking, with its immense potential for tourism, including budget travellers and stay home concept as in Ladakh or Kerala. Day-and-night service buses are frequent, though hotels are few. The innumerable streams and channels flowing from the north are ideal for backwater boating (as in Kerala) or adventure sports like boating and rafting, much better than the Ganga north of Rishikesh. Nature is unpolluted here. But industrialisation creates jobs, and it is a matter of time before industries come up here. But it is important that stringent pollution control measures are built in to avoid the horrors of industrial pollution.

Inland Water Transport and Ferries

There are only three bridges on the Brahmaputra at Dhubri, Guwahati and Tezpur. Another is being planned at Bogibeel north of Dibrugarh. The sense of isolation is pronounced as civil ferries are not as reliable as military ones. On civil ferries, the charges for a Bolero equivalent vehicle are Rs 750 and individual passengers on boats about Rs 60 each. In lean season and on account of changing riverbed profile due to heavy siltation, the boats often get stuck aground and need to be pushed. Any lowering of lean flow will make cross-Brahmaputra movement difficult.

NOTES

1. Seminar proceedings have since been published as an IDSA publication. See Pushpita Das and Namrata Goswami (eds.), *India's North East: New Vistas for Peace*, New Delhi: Manas, 2008.
2. I had served in Dahung, Sela, and Nurarong area of West Kameng district from 1971 to 1974. For operations in Bangladesh we had moved to Agartala via Guwahati and Shillong. Also occasional visits were paid to areas such as Tangla, Mangaldoi and Tezpur. The contrast and changes after over thirty years were very impressive and the field trip helped me in analysing environmental matters.
3. K.K. Baruah, "Environmental Challenges and Future Strategies". In Das and Goswami (eds.), *India's North East ...*, n. 1, pp. 156–66.
4. This part has been facilitated by excellent literature such as the *Arunachal Pradesh Human Development Report 2005*, The Forest Commission, websites of the Government of Arunachal Pradesh and those of the districts of North and West Siang, and Arunachal Tourism accessed in April 2007, at <http://arunachalpradesh.nic.in/aptribes.htm>, <http://uppersiang.nic.in>,<http:westsiang.nic.in>, <http://www.arunachaltourism.com/about.htm>. For the population of Buddhists, data were taken from *The First Report on Religion: Census of India, 2001*.
5. Verrier Elwin, *A Philosophy of NEFA*, with Foreword by the Prime Minister of India, Shillong, North East Frontier Agency, 1959, second revised edition.
6. Nari Rustomji, *Imperilled Frontiers: India's North East Borderlands*, New Delhi: Oxford University Press, 1989, pp. 143–4.
7. R.C. Srivastava and R.K. Choudhary, "Documentation of inherited

traditional knowledge of 110 ethnic communities of Arunachal Pradesh", *Current Science,* 92 (9) (10 May 2007): 1198.

8. Charudutt Mishra and Aparajita Datta, "A new bird species from Eastern Himalayan Arunachal Pradesh—India's biological frontier", *Current Science,* 92 (9) (10 May 2007): 1205–6. I also experienced this phenomenon during my travel by road over three days from the foothills to Tuting in Siang region.
9. A local viper, called *barta,* which in Nishi tribal dialect means the most poisonous, was discovered in November 2007. See *Hindustan Times* (New Delhi), 20 November 2007.
10. Ramachandra Guha, "Colonialism and Conflict in the Himalayan Forest". In Ramachandra Guha (ed.), *Social Ecology,* New Delhi: Oxford University Press, 1994, p. 288.
11. Other states having the Inner Line regulation are Nagaland and Mizoram.
12. E.P. Gee in his *The Wild Life of India* (London: Collins, 1964, p. 120) mentions that at Tuting one can see the snowy peaks of 25,445 feet high Namche Barwa. This is not possible as snowy peaks were indeed visible from Tuting but they were not the features of Namche Barwa.
13. Sanjib Baruah, *Policy Studies 33: Post frontier Blues: Towards a New Policy Framework for Northeast India,* Washington: East-West Center, 2007.
14. Erik de Maaker and Vibha Joshi, "Introduction: The Northeast and Beyond: Region and Culture", *South Asia: Journal of South Asian Studies,* XXX(3) (December 2007): 381–403.
15. When I gave a presentation of my field visit at IDSA in April 2007, opinions were divided on the concepts of Inner Line. This shows that the subject now needs to be researched and studied further in light of changed circumstances. Interestingly, the Governor Shri S.K. Singh in the Foreword to the *Arunachal Pradesh Human Development Report 2005* laments that "we have failed to structure adequate infrastructure for transport, roads, communications, and partly by refusing to abolish Inner Line Permit system which the colonial rulers had built to meet their own compulsions of security and requirements of economy and exclusivity of the last quarter of the 19th century."
16. R.K. Manhas, J.D.S. Negi, Rajesh Kumar and P.S. Chauhan, "Temporal Assessment of Growing Stock, Biomass and Carbon Stock of Indian Forests", *Climatic Change,* 74(1–3) (January 2006).
17. PS Ramakrishnan, " Sustainable Development of Jhum with Conversation of Biodiversity in North East India: Where Do We Stand?, *Man and Society: A Journal of North East Studies,* Vol. 1, No. 1, Spring 2004.
18. As quoted in "People's Forestry", *One India One People,* July 2003, p. 20.
19. Tiplut Nonbri, "Timber Ban in North East: Effect of Livelihood and Gender", *Economic and Political Weekly,* 26 May 2001: 1893–1900.

20. "Trees Are Our Only Livelihood", *Down to Earth,* 31 December 2004: 46.
21. Internet correspondence of 18 October 2006 with Rajesh Kumar (a statistician), n. 16.
22. Mihin Dollo, Prasanna K. Samal and Prabal Sen, "Shifting Cultivation and Conservation Issues in the Context of Prevention of Desertification of Arunachal Pradesh", *Man In India,* 87(3 & 4) (July–December 2007): 219–30.
23. *Ibid.*
24. A. Arunachalam, M.L. Khan and K. Arunachalam, "Balancing Traditional Jhum Cultivation with Modern Agroforestry in Eastern Himalaya: A biodiversity hot spot", *Current Science,* 83(2) (25 July 2002): 117–18.
25. P.S. Ramakrsihnan, "Sustainable Development of Jhum with Conservation of Biodiversity in North East India: Where Do We Stand?", *Man and Society,* 1(4) (Spring 2004), Indian Council of Social Science Research, North East Region, Shillong.
26. P.S. Ramakrsihnan, "Sustainable Mountain Development: The Himalayan tragedy", *Current Science,* 92(3) (10 February 2007): 308-16.
27. Arunachalam *et al.*, "Balancing Traditional Jhum Cultivation ...", n. 24. See my observation in Preface about the trend on the near-total absence of the young generation in agriculture in India.
28. *Arunachal Pradesh Human Development Report 2005,* pp. 169–70.
29. P. K. Gautam, " Sino- Indian Water Issues", *Strategic Analysis,* 32(6) (November—December 2008): 969-974.
30. Sunil Kumar Singh, M.M. Sarin and Christian France-Lanord, "Chemical Erosion in the Eastern Himalaya", *Geochimica et Cosmochimica Acta,* 69(14) (2005): 3573–88; and Sunil Kumar Singh, "Spatial Variability in Erosion in the Brahmaputra Basin: Causes and impacts", *Current Science,* 90(9) (10 May 200): 1272–6.
31. A Task Force to study the influence of Buddhism has been formed at the IDSA in 2008 to study these aspects(forthcoming).
32. Sanjib Baruah, *Durable Disorder: Understanding the Political Economy of the North East India,* New Delhi: Oxford University Press, 2005, pp. 71-2.
33. Paul Collier, "Economic Causes of Conflict and Their Implications for Policy". In Chester A. Crocker *et al.* (eds.), *Turbulent Peace: The Challenges of Managing International Conflicts,* Washington, DC: United States Institute of Peace, 2001, pp. 71-2.
34. *The Hindu* (New Delhi), 1 October 2006.
35. Amartaya Sen, *Identity and Violence: The Illusions of Destiny,* London: Allen Lane, 2006, p. 143.
36. Ugelvik Larsen, *Theory and Method in Political Science: First Steps to*

Synthesize a Discipline, Boulder: Social Science Monograph, New York: Columbia University Press, 2005, note p. 10.

37. Partha S. Ghosh, "Socio-Political Trends in Southern Asia: Security Implications for India", *Faultline,* Vol. 17, February 2006.
38. Full page advertisement, *Hindustan Times* (New Delhi), 21 September 2006 by Ministry of Power **<www.powermin.nic.in>**.
39. Linda Chhakchhuak, "Arunachal Pradesh: Development and Destruction", *The Hindu Survey of the Environment* 2006, pp. 79–85.
40. "Fissured Land", *Down to Earth,* 15 October 2006: 27–36.
41. John Briscoe and R.P.S. Malik, *India Water Economy: Bracing for a Turbulent Future,* New Delhi: Oxford University Press, 2006.
42. *Frontline,* 14 July 2006.
43. *Down to Earth,* 15 June 2005.
44. Shekhar Singh, "Ensuring Biological Security", *Comprehensive Security: A Comprehensive Security Dialogue Project,* New Delhi: Delhi Policy Group, 2004, pp. 148–85.
45. One initial hitch in the Nathu La trade was the insistence for production of PAN cards (which as per the Constitution is not required from persons of the North-East) by Commerce Ministry officials. This is one example of teething trouble in this inter-ministry exercise. This insight was provided by Professor Mahendra S. Lama during his presentation at the IDSA on the opening of Nathu La on 31 July 2006.
46. K.C. Kabra and R.K.P.G. Singha, "Emerging Trends and Future Prospects". In Davis Syiemlieh and Anuradha Dutta (eds.), *Challenges of Development in the North-East India,* New Delhi: Regency, 2006, Chapter 15.
47. *Ibid.* The authors mention 42 heroin conversion labs functioning in Myanmar, where acetic anhydride is smuggled from India.
48. As quoted by Wim van Spengen, *Tibetan Borders: A Geohistoric Analysis of Trade and Traders,* London: Keegan Paul International, 2000, pp. 98-102.
49. Prakash Tandon, *Punjabi Saga: 1857–2000,* New Delhi: Penguin Books, 1988.
50. In Assam, in some areas, paddy is cultivated in three cropping seasons known as *ahu, sali* and *boro*. Rain-fed *sali* is the main kharif crop and due to drought in the year 2006, marginal, and small farmers (who comprise 62 per cent) faced acute distress. See Sushant Talukdar, "Missing monsoon", *Frontline,* 6 October 2006, pp. 32–3. K.K. Baruah also mentions rain fed lowland and medium-land (*Sali* rice), irrigated (*Boro* rice), rain-fed up-land (*Ahu* rice) and deep-water (Bao rice) see K.K. Baruah, "Environmental Challenges and Future Strategies", in Das and Goswami (eds.), *India's North East ...,* n. 1, p. 163.
51. Elwin, *A Philosophy of NEFA,* n. 5.

Photograph 6.1: Suspension Bridge over Siang River.

Photograph 6.2: Siang River before it Enters India.

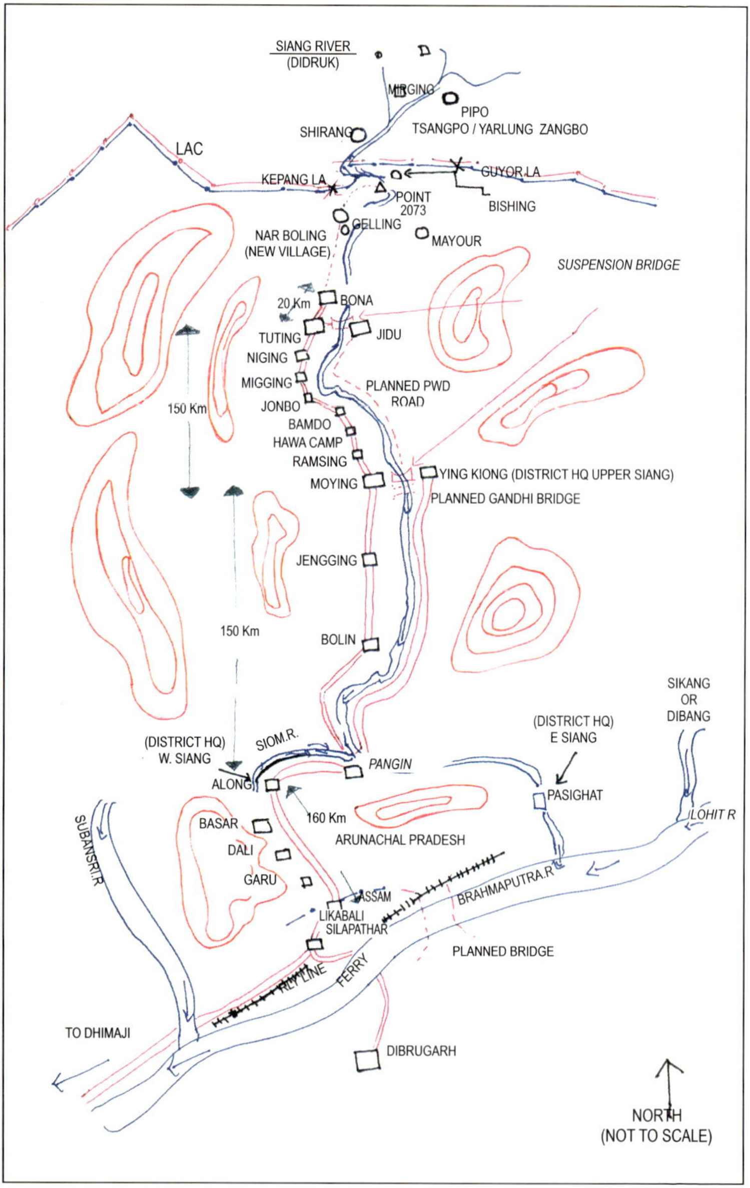

Sketch 6.1: Route from Dibrugarh till Gelling.

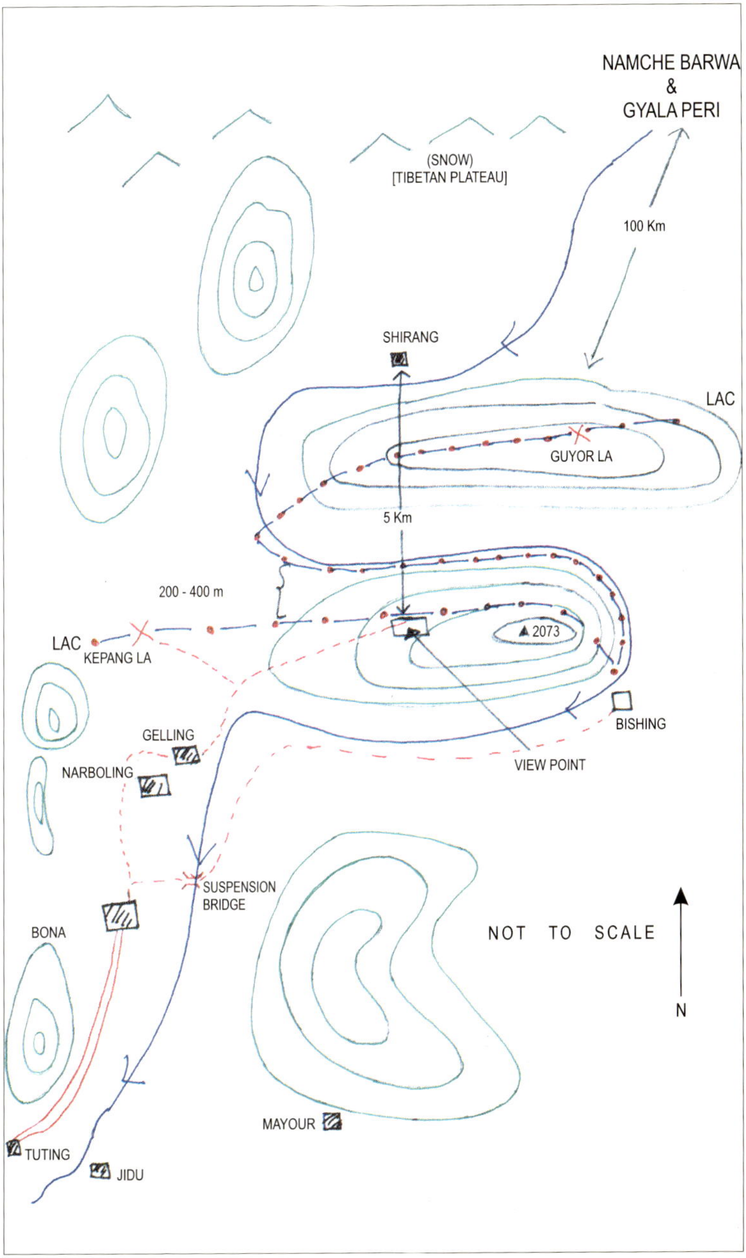

Sketch 6.2: Route from Tuting to Gelling and View Point at Base of Point 2073.

7

Identifying Threats, Challenges and Opportunities

This chapter attempts to evaluate the emerging ecological threats, what the future would look like and what roles and tasks can the ETF perform in general. It also includes aspects which the military needs to include in its routines. Though the starting point is ecological restoration by the military, the ideas can also be applied to any segment of society. Performance, after all, is a national effort.

Emerging Ecological Threats

The ecological threats that have emerged as the population multiplies are as a result of two reasons. One, which is currently a long-term challenge and not much in the public consciousness, is the overload of greenhouse gases in the atmosphere which have been emitted by humans ever since the Industrial Revolution as a result of the use of fossil fuel, land use change and deforestation. This has led to the phenomenon of climate change which is visiting us as global warming with dire consequences. The second reason or the source is extraction of minerals and other manmade changes on the land surface of the earth due to urbanisation, infrastructure building, soil erosion, energy generation, over-exploitation of water bodies and non-biodegradable waste stream due to massive agriculturisation, industrialisation and chemicalisation. Restoring of natural capital becomes difficult or is not allowed to take place due to the need to feed a growing population and provisioning of material needs from a finite land resource. While salinity, waterlogging and desertification due to improper irrigation or deforestation or mineral extraction is an old problem, the newly emerging climate change is a serious threat affecting national and international security.

Scientific consensus has established that global warming has begun. The average surface air temperature in most of India has risen by half a degree centigrade during the second half of the twentieth century and by one degree in the Himalayas.

What are the reasons for the looming ecological threats? One reason is the concept of "development" itself combined with our obsession with "growth" of mainstream economic tools such as gross domestic product (GDP) at all costs. We know that GDP = consumption + investment + government expenditure + net exports (exports minus imports). But it does not account for say jobless growth (also called joyless growth) or the ecosystem services.

While growth is essential for a developing country it hides many truths. Without going into arguments on the critique of growth it is sufficient to state that according to the World Bank, the cost of environmental degradation in China is 8 per cent in GDP terms. For India it is in the region of 4.5 to 8 per cent.[1] Gross Natural Product has not yet been factored into mainstream economic planning. Thus we find that to restore the ecology after an economic activity, we need to spend money. At times the damage may be so severe that recovery may not be possible. This is called the "Humpty Dumpty Effect".[2] This is the crux of the dilemma between development and the environment. Mainstream economists argue that in the initial phases pollution rises but as income increases environmental matters start getting addressed. This is called the Environmental Kuznets Curve (EKC), which in other words is an empirical relation purporting to show that with ongoing growth in GDP, pollution at first increases but then reaches a maximum and declines.[3] EKC may not always be true. How do we relate it to the falling quality of Himalayan ecology, the shrinking of the deltas and other scars?

Ecological events or over-use of resources, which have a potential to become emerging threats are:

(a) *Degradation of Himalayan Ecology*: Abnormal and accelerated melting of Himalayan glaciers leading to glacial lake outburst floods, floods in the plains followed by drought and conversion of perennial rivers to seasonal.
(b) *Soil Degradation* due to wind and water erosion, excess chemicalisation, waterlogging and salinity leading to challenges to food security.
(c) *Loss of Biodiversity*: Deforestation, habitat loss and intrusive alien species.
(d) *Coastal Regions and Marine Pollution*: Degradation of coastal regions, mangrove forests, coral reefs due to human action compounded by sea-level rise. In the short term, the intensity of extreme weather events like cyclone would increases.
(e) *Wetlands*: Loss of wetlands, lakes, talabs, johars and ponds that provided silent but vital ecosystem services.
(f) *Desertification* can spiral out of control as a result of degradation of forests and land due to ill-planned mining, ill-planned irrigation and agricultural practices and deforestation.
(g) *Wasteland*: Wasteland in India is 20.7 per cent of land area. Identifying wasteland in the country is no easy task. B.B. Vohra points out that in the past only deforestation was emphasised and non-forested wasteland was ignored.[4] Clear-cut division of wasteland is not a simple task. To a corporate eye it is a resource ideally suited for commercial farming. To the military it is an ideal area for collective training. In our planning we tend to ignore village commons like pastures as grazing lands or wood lots which perform common property resource functions.[5] Many conflicts now seem to originate in the classification of land and what is common. Increasingly, human security angle is being brought into these matters.

Therefore, a thorough and transparent classification and understanding of forest, revenue, common or village land is necessary. Eco-restoration of wasteland in many of its facets is an emerging task. Identification of the right area(s) and people's participation would now form important inputs to ETF projects in the future.

(h) *Urbanisation*: It is surprising that urbanisation has been listed as a threat. The reason for it being a threat to the ETF community is that "in the good old days" most of the troops were from the villages with a rustic and agrarian upbringing. Digging, fieldwork, ploughing, de-weeding the fields and other nuances associated with agriculture were second nature. They were also well versed with animal husbandry matters. Now with urbanisation to reach half of India by 2047 the "green fingers" expected from the troops cannot be taken for granted. This is like losing our gene pool of biodiversity in crops and cattle. A strategy would need to be worked out in order not to forget activities linked directly to Nature and the traditional wisdom that accompanies it. Without a centre of excellence no comprehensive plan to implement a vision future of ETF would be possible. Institutionally we need to capture and record our actions, literature and results in order not to forget our traditional green wisdom.

(i) *Waste*: The generation of waste by human activity is now beyond the capacity of the biosphere to absorb or recycle. The atmosphere is getting overburdened with greenhouse gases leading to climate change. The lithosphere and hydrosphere are getting chemicalised by industrial and civic waste. Rivers have become sewage drains.

(j) *Extraction Industry*: Industrialisation, mining of mineral resources, and physical infrastructure building consume resources which do not regenerate on their own barring biomass. Sustainable development in this sector would also demand acknowledgement of the ground realities of the process by which the impact of mining on the environment is repaired.[6] This includes topsoil management

The *UN Millennium Ecosystem Assessment Report 2005* has concluded that the challenge of reversing the degradation of ecosystems while meeting increasing demands for their services can be partially met under some scenarios, but these involve significant changes in policies, institutions, and practices that are not currently underway. Many options exist to conserve or enhance specific ecosystem services in ways that reduce negative trade-offs or that provide positive synergies with other ecosystem services.[7]

Perhaps, one initiative that does not need any social engineering or change of modern lifestyle is planting trees. We know that the national environmental policy specifies that 33 per cent of the country's plains and 66 per cent hills/ mountains need to be under forest cover by 2025. At present the state of forests is 20.55 per cent (with dense cover 12.68% and open 7.87%). If the infantry is the queen of battle in a shooting-war, the tree is the queen of battle against environmental degradation.

An Emerging Role for ETF

With nearly 55,000 servicemen retiring each year, there is a disciplined human resource. Studies by the Centre for Science and Environment have shown that the maximum gainful employment is in the field of eco-generation.[8] Seeing the success of the experiments with an ETF, strong policy prescriptions for a logical and massive expansion of ETF have been articulated by political leaders.[9] In his Presidential Address in the Second Darbari Seth Memorial Lecture in August 2006, the then Defence Minister highlighted that the men in uniform were all committed environmentalists. You can tell a military settlement from a distance. He then elaborated on the ETF as the saviour of the Himalayas. He told the audience that he had suggested to the Prime Minister to set up a trans-Himalayan authority to save the Himalayas and the project would be operational very soon.[10] Future roles, besides plantation of trees, could be in disaster management, social development, sanitation and ecological and environmental roles.[11] The subsequent paragraphs identify and suggest some new tasks for the ETF for the future.

Formal Training

The Report of the National Forest Commission had recommended "formal training institutes where civil servants and armed forces are trained, need to incorporate forest and wildlife conservation as an important aspect of their induction training programme, as well as in-service training programmes".[12] Its seminal contribution the Forest Commission has attempted to institutionalise as a national effort, to involve both the military and the paramilitary. The Commission notes:

> Armed and paramilitary forces deployed on the nation's borders have effective control over vast habitats that are critical to a number of montane and other species. Their active involvement in the conservation of these areas would not only prevent poaching by these personnel themselves as has been the case in the past, but will prevent poaching and habitat degradation by others, prevent illegal transit of wildlife products and will provide periodic data to the wildlife authorities concerned as to the status and distribution of a large number of taxa about which very little is known. Similarly, if sensitized, the Air Force and the Navy could also be of invaluable help in this regard, to both carry out surveys in remote areas and to prevent illegal traffic in wildlife products. The Army has set up a special unit called the Environment and Ecology Cell, which deals with conservation aspects. It has been in touch with the MoEF for a number of years. It would be appropriate if MoEF, the cell and concerned State Governments work out collaborative projects in different selected areas for long-term conservation efforts, involving strict protection of areas and species, especially endangered species, their

> status surveys, and the prevention of the passage of illegal wildlife trade.[13]

The Commission then comes to the core of the issue on the link of military and environment:

> The Indian Army today is one of the largest landholders in the country with establishments located in different ecosystems and biogeographic zones. Their locations, deployment, and nature of duty, binds them with land and nature. Today, the real estate of the Army comprises 62 cantonments, 192 military stations, depots/training establishments, manoeuvre areas, firing ranges and military farms. The Indian Army is deployed in many areas rich in ecological diversity, like the Rann of Kutch, the Thar Desert, the length and breadth of the Himalaya, the tropical rain forests of northeast India, the Western Ghats and the Andaman and Nicobar Islands. This and the fact that the bulk of the manpower is recruited from rural areas, gives the jawan an edge in understanding nature and the intricate web of life. The very organizational structure, training, motivation, discipline inter-communications and mobility, make the Army ideally suited for environmental protection, when not otherwise employed on the prime task of national security.[14]

Perhaps the Commission overlooked the urbanisation trend and the fact that no longer soldiers will be farmers as in the past. This indicates a strong public imagination on the ethos of the army to retain this knowledge.[15]

Raising of a Centre of Excellence and Expansion

There is a need to have a centre of excellence where future ecological tasks could be projected. This will be better than the existing and reactive way where we do a firefight after an event. Perhaps the Delhi government's decision to raise a company for compensatory reforestation as a result of national highway construction is the right type of proactive approach. There is a need for the ETF arm of the TA (with the support of the Ministry of Defence) in coordination with the

Ecological Cell of the Quartermasters Branch and Army Training Command to gear up to take up this challenge. The job would be to get involved as stakeholders in an Environmental Impact Assessment (EIA). An EIA of India on account of an 8 per cent GDP growth till the year 2020 would indicate areas where serious ecological degradation may occur. Not all cost-benefit analyses would point to termination of a developmental project. However, this exercise would make the process more nuanced and transparent. It would indicate areas where ETF-like units may need to deploy during the planning stage itself.

National Cadet Corps

Another avenue that can be used to spread the gospel of ecological restoration to the youth of the country is via the resource of National Cadet Corps (NCC). The NCC has performed yeoman service in nearly all fields of national integration. Besides doing drill and firing practices, NCC cadets can be given a modified capsule on ecological restoration. Their syllabus could be suitably changed with changing circumstances.

Vector-borne Diseases

In a study which praises the services being rendered by the ETF, demographer Ashish Bose has suggested that monitoring and surveillance of vector-borne diseases like malaria, filaria, kala azar, dengue and Japanese encephalitis in the emerging malarial region of Rajasthan would be best performed by ETF.[16] Another threat is the forthcoming bird 'flu pandemic, in which 150-200 million deaths world-wide are projected. Swine flu is another similar pandemic. It is unlikely that our infectious disease surveillance mechanism at the national level is ready to take on this disaster. The concept of raising medical ETF in such disasters may be of help. The armed forces were requisitioned to combat the mosquito-borne viral disease chikungunya and dengue in Kerala in 2007.[17]

Water Hyacinth

The Harike head works in the Punjab as also the Jamuna at Kalindikunj get choked with water hyacinth (Eichhornia Crassipes). It is not the routine work of the regular army to clear it. But the ETF and the Indian military have a number of good practices. The idea needs to be sold to state governments to raise ETF with an assurance that it would also have unemployed youth on the rolls.

An ETF raised clearing the water hyacinth can also assist in providing raw material for simple furniture, as Thailand is doing. Another innovation is bioremediation. The plant grows rapidly when nutrients are available. It acts as a bio-indicator of pollution. Used with innovation it can be used as a bio-remedial method for open sewage drains in urban areas, provided it is monitored and removed regularly to be used as compost. An ETF can perform this municipal body's job as it would solve the problem of urban liquid waste and provide better human health and security.

Political Economy of Rag-pickers

Urban solid waste disposal is another area of concern with limited landfills. Much of recyclable solid waste is picked up by the unorganised and poor rag-pickers. The magnitude of the problem is phenomenal. Is the nation prepared to segregate the waste of urban areas and use it productively? The task is massive and needs the discipline of a military organisation. The most pressing problem is the absence of landfill sites. Even existing landfill sites are a threat as persistent pollutants leach into the groundwater and make the groundwater like slow-acting poison. Each city can organise the unemployed labour force of slum dwellers under a group of municipal workers under ETF leadership. This organisation can become profit-making by making recycled raw material like polymers/plastic bags for extraction of hydrocarbons, compost manures, and feedstock for power plants. Part of the profit can be utilised to educate the rag-pickers.

Reclaiming Returns from the Kyoto Protocol CDM

Trees are carbon sinks. Over the last decade the ETF has planted two crore plants. Tree planting projects of the ETF must be processed through proper channels to get carbon credits and thus funds to budget more ETFs. Till April 2008, not a single project has been claimed by any government organisation.[18] Only the private sector has taken business advantage of it.[19] This probably has something to do with the culture inherited by government departments from the pre-economic liberalisation era. It is time the government departments and the armed forces take some lead in this challenge.[20] One important suggestion during the climate change conference at Bali in December 2007 was on a concept of Reducing Emissions from Deforestation and Degradation (REDD). Degrading and destroyed forests are responsible for approximately 20 per cent of greenhouse gas emissions. Post-Kyoto period or beyond 2012, this REDD may take a more concrete form. It is important to get our data and information ready in order to benefit from this concept.

An Expanded ETF

From the above it can be concluded that besides the existing ETFs which are performing the core job of planting trees, special ETFs may need to be raised to perform special jobs such as disaster management, turning waste to energy, cleaning water bodies of water hyacinth, disease surveillance, and so on. This chapter cannot go into the nuts and bolts of the organisation as the one-size-fits-all formula may not apply. However, it is hoped that the idea would be taken to its logical conclusion for implementation. What is more, even our neighbouring countries can organise ETFs for restoration of the fragile border regions.

Some Ecological Issues for Consideration

Vilayati vs. Desi Kikar

Sand dune stabilisation in Rajasthan has been done with

intrusive species such as vilayati kikar. The species has spread on non-sand dune areas, evicting the eco-friendly desi kikar. In most towns and cities in north India including Delhi, vilayati kikar has been grown or planted. Pradip Krishen in his seminal work *Trees of Delhi: A Field Guide* (New Delhi: Dorling Kindersley, 2006, p. 38) pointed out that afforestation of the Delhi ridge in 1914 to 1929 was done with vilayayti kikar. Today people mistake it for babool or desi kikar. Vilayati kikar is the principal cause of extinction of a number of native species.

There is a need to establish the trend and develop a strategy by the military in border areas and peace stations to plant the right mix of trees. Desi kikar has its use in diets for recuperating patients and pregnant women. Its flower is used to treat insanity, its bark dust for snakebite. The wood is used for stationery and furniture. Kikar gum makes excellent glue. Vilayati kikar has no such attributes.

A consolidated effort covering the entire country may be required. The work involved may require generating the type of trees planted by ETF and those existing in military stations, cantonments and other areas under charge of the military. An analysis would need to be made of the required type of changes and improvements. Areas where ecologically unsuited trees have been planted need to be reforested with ecologically suited trees, ideally endemic to the region. A case which is yet to be resolved by scientific methods is the problem of trees linked to rainfall in the cold desert such as Ladakh. One such case is given at Appendix 1.

Intrusive Species in Andaman and Nicobar Islands

A team from the Centre for Environmental Management of Degraded Ecosystem (CEMDE), School of Environmental Studies, University of Delhi has warned that in Choura island of the Andaman and Nicobar group one needs to look out for a certain shrub that grows in tropical forests and is an invasive species. Earlier the shrub had limited growth because it was denied sunlight by the islands' tree canopy, but with trees perishing in the tsunami, the shrubs have multiplied and slowed the growth of new trees.[21] This demands that the intrusive specie must be removed manually. But manpower may not be readily available in that region. Such silent emergencies therefore need a proactive strategy. If we wait for the state government to be convinced of a project after a few years by then the damage would have been done and would have spread out of control. Untying the slow knots of bureaucracy and procedures and getting a faster response is considered an important vision for ETF deployment. Prevention is better than cure.

Biofuel

Biofuel plants such as jatropha have entered the public domain due to oil and energy shortages. Some experiments need to be done on its ecological sustainability under intensive cropping. Military land may be earmarked for this experiment. If ecologically suitable, fuel for crucial military equipment can be provided by an infrastructure that already exists under the Quartermaster General and the Army Service Corps which deals with all aspects of fuel, oil and lubricants. The liquid fuel may also be required to operate military equipment if oil (fossil fuel) shortages are encountered and no substitute to mainstream fossil fuel has been found as a replacement

Congress Grass (Parthenium)

The military makes a conscious effort to remove congress grass in military stations as a routine. According to scientists at CEMDE, the physical removal needs to be done before flowering. Flowering also varies from region to region. A flowering plant should not be touched as the seeds may spread rapidly.[22] This knowledge may not be widely available. The military can revisit the methodologies to tackle the menace and help the nation establish good practices for civil society to emulate.

Disseminating Ecological Knowledge

After the 1962 Sino-Indian war a General Staff pamphlet "Edible Wild Plants of the Himalayas" was produced for survival training. It is still a masterpiece of coordinated work by our scientific community for the defence forces. We need to have pamphlets on simple arboriculture plans which should guide the working party commanders in jobs such as clearing of congress grass (parthenium), reasons why not to plant water-guzzling and ecologically harmful eucalyptus trees, guidelines to identify and report harmful intrusive species, and so on. The aim is to implement a professional long-term strategy to plant the correct type of tree suited to the ecology and climate of the region, such as desi kikar. Ecological wisdom that needs to be spread by the scientific and ecological community needs to be included to be implemented in a dedicated and disciplined manner by the defence forces.

Corporate Social Responsibility

We are now witness to the phenomenon of "creative destruction".[23] Corporate Social Responsibility (CSR) is the new mantra where ecological matters also need to be looked into. The private sector with its creative energies can help in greening India and simultaneously provide employment. Investing in clean technologies and proper waste disposal by itself is a great achievement. However, it needs to have incentives. Adam Smith's "Invisible Hand" needs to be related to ecological restoration in a market—and consumer-driven economy. The need for profits and growth at many places conflicts with the environmental aims. Initially, green initiatives may imply a drag on the profit margins. But the energies and capacities of corporate India to perform are immense; it can do much better than resorting to the gimmickry of painting boulders in the Himalayas with green paint. The government also may need to take a macro-policy decisions and regulate this endeavour with a Keynesian touch. The Foreword to the *United Nations Human Development Report 2007/2008* by the heads of UNDP and UNEP, in referring to climate change, mentions that the "benefits are likely to be realised through Keynesian and Schumpeterian mechanism with new incentives for massive investment stimulating overall demand and creative destruction leading to innovation and productivity jumps in a wide array of sectors".[24]

Educating the Children

The Supreme Court has given a ruling that environmental issues are to be included in the school syllabus. In the wisdom of the pedagogic community, chapters on disaster management have been included. Probably, mixing up a topic such as environment to young minds, already under pressure with other subjects would have led to inhibition and reduced performance in examinations. We all are consumers with expectations. How can I say that there is a problem of ecology when I as an adult in urban India have a substantial ecological footprint? I attempted to place the children as a part of the solution when I interacted with them. This made me think and I wrote a piece "Teaching Global Environmental Change while Overcoming Guilt", reproduced at Appendix 2 to this chapter.

Conclusion

This chapter has agued that serious ecological degradation has set in, which needs to be checked. This stems from humanity's excess emission from fossil fuel on its path of industrialisation. The primary process is unsustainable use of natural resources. The new threat riding piggyback over it is global warming. Besides, the demand for minerals and wood and the material consumption of the economic trajectory leads to environmental problems.

Terrain-specific strategies can be worked out from the chapters dealing with the regions. Also, the larger issues that have been illuminated must be faced and dealt with. Placing the overall problem in perspective the chapter has shown how the unique institution of the ETF of the Indian Army has been successfully executing ecological tasks in remote and difficult terrain and conditions. This success needs to be reinforced with a national movement to raise many more ETF-type of units for not only afforestation but other emerging ecological challenges. With a steady stream of ex-servicemen more number of ETFs can be organised to restore our natural capital. This model can be suitably adapted by society at large, including the paramilitary organisations, government departments and the private sector under CSR.

APPENDIX 1

THE CASE OF LADAKH

Brigadier N.B. Patel in his piece "Indian Army and Green Governance: Action Plan for Ladakh" in the Bombay Natural History Society (BNHS) Green Governance web site, accessed in August 2005, concludes that

> The delicate ecological balance should not be disturbed due to over enthusiasm and over ensurance (sic). Indiscriminate afforestation would also impact the cold desert ecosystems. Already, many apprehensions have been raised about the impact of afforestation and one of the perceived effects is the increase in rainfall in the last few years.

The BNHS awarded the Green Governance Award to 8 Infantry Division in February 2006 for greening the Kargil region. This led to a series of letters and interviews.

Opening Correspondence: to BNHS, 2 March 2006

Dear Director/Editor BNHS,

I am very keen to get some research papers and scientific inputs to an issue which has not been resolved. Vide Brig NB Patel's piece on Ladakh, he has rightly cautioned that indiscriminate afforestation impacts on the cold desert ecosystem. Dr Stobdan, a senior fellow with us who hails from Ladakh confirms that trees in Leh region planted under the aegis of DRDO and army have changed precipitation from snow to rain. This has a negative side. In the *Sainik Samachar* of 1-15 February 2006, it is reported that 8 Mountain Division has been awarded the BNHS Green Governance Award in Kargil region. I would be grateful if a study and analysis be done or if not then be sponsored by you to see the ecological impact. Also type of trees may be important. This may have to be seen in the larger framework of climate change and warming and changes in precipitation. Probably the intensity of rain could be a result of climate change or it could well be trees?

This knowledge may be helpful in preparing greening plans by the military in the future.

With warm regards, etc.

BNHS replied, 2 March 2006:

Thank you very much for bringing out the issue of tree plantation in Ladakh. This issue was brought to my notice by many people when I visited Ladakh in June 2005, but I am not very sure whether there is direct relationship between better tree cover and more rainfall. More rains, if this is true, could be due to climate change or decadal cycle in precipitation. This needs to be studied. Lots of people think that more trees bring more rain but rainfall is determined by many factors on a much larger scale. I am not a climatologist so I cannot write more than this. Nevertheless, I agree with you that we need more studies to know the impact of increased tree plantation on the weather of Ladakh. In BNHS we do not have any expert to study this but you have stimulated me to think of the scientific project on this aspect. Let me discuss it with my colleagues who have more knowledge of the Ladakh region. I need your permission to forward your email to my colleagues.

Best wishes.

Asad R. Rahmani, Director, BNHS.

Views of GOC 8 Infantry Division of 23 March 2006 (Telephonic Interview)

The correspondence was passed on to GOC 8 Mountain Division for his views. Following is the gist:

(a) Green cover in the region about 0.1 per cent.
(b) There are five massive ranges in the Ladakh region. It is not possible to plant trees on those heights.
(c) Trees and the like providing building material, fuel, herbs, medicinal plants are being planted.

(d) Dr Ahmad of the DRDO at Leh conducts training of the military personnel charged with this task.
(e) In the past the Forest Department of Jammu and Kashmir used to give about Rs 4 per plant as incentive for forestation.
(f) Tree plantation has a very high socio-economic advantage.
(g) It is unlikely that rain pattern has changed due to this reason.

A Supplementary View

Pervez Dewan, who served as Resident Commissioner of Jammu and Kashmir in Delhi, comments about the subject of ecology in Jammu and Kashmir in *Jammu, Kashmir and Ladakh: Ladakh* (New Delhi: Manas, 2004, p. 90), as follows:

> After the 1960s the government went in for a massive plantation of trees. By the mid-1970s Ladakh's climate had begun to change. This cold desert had never known floods before, but in 1977, just one inch of rainfall caused a flood of sorts. The little snow that the plains of Leh receive is dry and flaky. But in autumn (not winter) of 1998 parts of Leh received snow that was at the same time wet, plentiful (almost a foot) and unusually early. This snow damaged many buildings, notably the Spituk monastery.

In a footnote he explains:

> The enormous increase in the number of trees since 1960s is a fact. So is the change in the climate. And yet there might be no common connection between the two. According to one school of thought, the climate begins to change only after 30 per cent of an area has been covered with trees. Neither Leh nor Kargil is anywhere near that figure. The change in climate in both districts could possibly be part of the overall change that has taken place in the Indian Himalayas and parts of central Asia, especially since 1998.[25]

Research Now Sought for Ladakh

The BNHS has promised to look into the matter. The aim is that the military in coordination with the local Forest Department plants the correct type of trees from the point of view of ecology in the long term and not just the trees that may be fast growing and easily available but ecologically harmful.

APPENDIX 2

TEACHING GLOBAL ENVIRONMENTAL CHANGE WHILE OVERCOMING GUILT

Talking of global environmental change, it is difficult not to feel "guilty" of being part of the problem. The pedagogical dilemma is that there is a gap between what I teach or the normative goals I propound and what I do. Here I will share some thoughts on being torn in the pincers of being a part of the problem and attempts to be a part of the solution.

Driving down for a presentation in a seminar, or flying to attend a meeting or for a field trip to study environmental change makes one aware what double standards are about. Everyday I consume fossil fuel with a global warming potential, to move from place A to B. Could it not be avoided? By my signature or ecological footprint am I not contributing to the surplus greenhouse gases residing now in the atmosphere? I am also a consumer of material. Material which, like this computer on which I type has taken a vast amount of energy, material and water. I upgrade my computer or replace a part, which is non-biodegradable. In doing so, toxic e-waste piles up for disposal in shrinking landfills. In teaching global environmental change surges of guilt appear and reappear. Most of the reasons for global environmental degradation are the very waste stream that I generate. These double standards give rise to guilt.

While interacting and giving presentations to matured audiences on topics such as "the challenges of development and environment" or "environmental security", it is easier to convince them about the helplessness of these "double standards". Introducing the subject, I will say that we cannot become hermits and shun worldly material benefits. There are two important aspects in consumerism. One is want satisfaction and the other is want limitation. Although I want to limit my demand, I am sort of helpless to influence the waste that accompanies a new shirt that I buy in a cardboard wrapper and plastic sheet. With competing market forces, attractive packaging is essential for sale. So many people depend on the consumer culture. If I stop buying, I am contributing to someone else's poverty. So, in spite of being frugal and limiting my wants, I contribute in some way to the waste stream and the accompanying climate change. To overcome guilt, I take recourse to trends—what is the tendency in the other people. Sociologists say that in many developed societies a few decades ago families without a car were considered poor. Now, the family is considered poor if the father and the son do not own a car each.

But when interacting with schoolchildren and teachers, like that of an eco-club, the discourse undergoes a shift. This is the shift: when teaching global environmental change is posed to schoolchildren, the first thing that strikes is—Am I part of the problem or am I part of the solution? Chief Seattle of the native American Suquamish tribe has a view on this: "The Earth does not belong to man; man belongs to Earth. Man did not weave the web of life: he is merely a strand in it. We do not inherit the Earth from our ancestors; *we borrow it from our children.*"

Great care needs to be exercised when teaching global environmental change to children. If the children are from the poor strata, who would rather work as rag-pickers or help their parents in agricultural work, they would be the least interested in what I have to say. One needs to be sensitive to this reality. Children of poor people are struggling to survive. If they are from the rural background, then their traditional ecological knowledge is better than mine. If they are rag-pickers from urban slums, then their knowledge of domestic waste is far superior to mine. The little boy grazing his goats will not be impressed with data saying that the goat population which grazes is far in excess of biomass production of a given piece of grazing land or a common property resource.

So, how do I begin interacting with urban children of an eco-club of an elite school? I must confess to them in the beginning: children are not part of the mess; the adults are. Me and my ancestors have created the problem of climate change due to mostly fossil-fuel-based energy and land-use change since the beginning of the Industrial Revolution. But now, as children, we all need to become a part of the solution.

I tell them that our economic practices, like excessive burning of fossil fuel, the need for extractive resources, rapid population growth and rising expectations, require a fine balance. We need to do something about it. The first thing is to connect with nature. Great minds have reminded us, "Eating is an agricultural act". So I tell them: that as we prosper and have spending power, we reduce our cereal consumption and transfer that to consumption of dairy products, vegetables and fruits. Some other tips which I can provide are under three broad heads of religion and culture, what to do at school, and individual behaviour. I then realise that while teaching about these simple things, I am also motivated to change my habits and attitudes.

Religion and Culture

In the Hindu scriptures, the gods and the goddesses represent the environment. The goddess of Earth is Bhu-devi or Prithvi, also called Gaia by modern Western biologists. Water (Ap), Fire (Agni), Wind (Vayu) are gods and goddesses. The god of the sea is Varuna, and rain and thunder are Indra. Animals and their hybrids are also worshipped as gods—like the monkey god Hanuman or Ganesha the elephant-headed god. The sacred chants refer to bhu (Earth), bhuvah (Atmosphere), and sva (the Sky). The Persian word abadi, which now is part of Urdu and Hindi, was derived from ab (water), meaning settlement or civilisation. This is a good link to relate water with civilisation.

Other religions also have ecological messages. The web sites linking religion and environment of prestigious universities such as Harvard note that in the Holy Koran the Earth is mentioned 453 times and the sky 320 times. Prophet Mohammad said, "When doomsday comes, if someone has a palm shoot in his hand he should plant it".

The First Book of Moses, Genesis Chapter 1, BC 4004, notes: "28. And God blessed them and God said unto them, Be fruitful, and multiply, and replenish the earth, and subdue it, and have dominion over the fish of the sea, and over the fowl over the air, and over every living thing that moves upon the earth".

This was interpreted as meaning that man must master and subjugate Nature. Lynn White's famous essay of 1967 in *Science* laid the blame for environmental deterioration on religion. This is being revisited. The very fact that the Judaeo-Christian West is leading in establishing linkages between peace and environment shows that the time has come to have a fresh look at dogmas. We need to read the scriptures in context.

The Dhamma Sutra of the Buddhists is a treatise on ecology. The Bishnois of Rajasthan live on ecological principles. They preserve wildlife and trees; they bury the dead to save on fuelwood; and they are strict vegetarians. The Jains go to the extent of not even harming germs and insects and make a conscious effort for non-violence.

Finding Solution as Students

The second step in teaching global environmental change to children is to identify some solutions to the problem. As they continue with their studies they need to relate the academic discipline to the real world. Some simple solutions to the problem could be:

(a) The need to develop and understand the interdisciplinary nature of the subject as students and good citizens. This implies that when studying chemistry, geography or biology we must try and relate it to the water, carbon, and nitrogen cycles in nature. It is for us to find out if our waste is being absorbed by nature. If not, there is a problem for which social or technological solutions need to be found.

(b) We cannot discard ecological traditions based on ancient wisdom. There is a need to understand social ecology from the perspective of "How is ecology embedded in our traditions like sacred groves, religion, and in rural economy?"

(c) Perhaps, one easier way is to develop a capacity to discriminate between need and greed. We need to control greed.

(d) As students, we must develop compassion for the poor. Environmental changes are mostly adverse and severe, like floods and drought. The poor are the most vulnerable. As Nobel laureate Amartya Sen has mentioned, as long as we share guilt for the poor we will not neglect them. This compassion would need sprouting later in life as leaders and decision-makers in business, management, and (for some) politics.

(e) As students, to cope with challenges as a result of global environmental change we need to use science and technology keeping our local problems in mind.

(f) One simple operation directly linked to preservation is planting of trees. But planting trees is easy, their survival and maintenance is the real challenge. We must target more than 80 per cent survival rate and we must plant the right ecologically suitable tree.

(g) Finally, students must remember not to just clean our own homes. We will do well to connect with where does the waste go? Waste must either get dispersed without harm or absorbed or used as an input for another process. If the cycle is closed, then it is fine. But an open-ended waste cycle would lead to adverse change. For this we need to treat society as important as the self, home or family.

Solution at the School

Organised activities at school also provide a good forum to bring one closer to Nature and help in ecology. One threat is loss of biodiversity due to over-extraction of medicinal plants. Planting a herbal garden in school using organic manure and bio-fertilisers is one good idea for urban children to realise the value of plant life.

Other activities could be for schoolchildren to participate in the audit of use of water, energy and waste control on their campus.

Getting familiar with biodiversity is important. We need

to develop the art of watching flora and fauna in our daily lives. We are losing biodiversity before its discovery. One of the easiest ways to be a part of the solution in environmental change is to record the types of plants, trees, birds and insects. Also, one must look out for the vanishing vultures and report any sighting. We also must be on the lookout for vanishing frogs. Intrusive species are the second-biggest cause of loss of biodiversity after habitat loss (as a result of deforestation). We must develop an eye for them in our regions. Congress grass (Parthenium), water hyacinth (Eichhornia crassipes) and lantana are a few of such intrusive alien species that need to be removed from the campus and also from residential areas.

Individual Ecology and Health

Finally, in teaching global environmental change we need to understand that adverse environmental change, besides degrading the natural ecosystem is affecting our health and internal ecosystem. Though the mortality rate has dropped and average life expectancy at birth is increasing, it does not mean that we are healthier now. Some ideas that need to be put into practice are:

(a) *Develop healthy eating habits*. Avoid junk food, which only caters to the taste-buds. The water crisis is upon us as agriculture with its water-intensive crops uses nearly 80 to 90 per cent water. If water is virtually embedded in rice then we can help in solving the problem by choosing to eat cereals which need less water like coarse grains (millet and sorghum) which have a higher nutrient content than rice.

(b) Fight a battle against the spread of lifestyle diseases due to environmental factors like urbanisation and sedentary lifestyle. Walk more. Building muscles only by gym workout is not enough. Develop stamina by running and playing games. Be regular about exercise.

Conclusion

Though all of us are consumers, we need to be conscious of our consumerist acts and the limits which we need to define. The poor need no such lessons; it is the rich and the privileged urbanites who need to be exposed to the problem of how adverse environmental change is impacting us. The adults need to accept the blame for the problem. Teaching adults should make them aware that they are a part of the problem. No purpose would be served if we confuse the children by placing them as a part of the problem. Rather, the children should be exposed to the way that they can be a part of the solution. Global environmental change also demands a change in thinking. By these simple methods, it is hoped that the future adults would be able to come to grips with the adverse impact of environmental change and make the planet a better place to live in.

Teaching also influences the teacher. Those sensitive or conscious of the guilt of being part of the problem of adverse global environmental change can volunteer to become teachers and can now help in reversing the trend.

NOTES

1. The World Bank, *Promoting Environmental Sustainability in Development: An Evaluation of the World Bank's Performance*, World Bank Evaluation Department(OED), Washington, DC: The World Bank, 2002, p. 15.
2. Andrew Simms, *Ecological Debt*, mentioned by Larry Elliot in the *Guardian Weekly*, 20-26 May 2005.
3. Herman E. Daly, "Economics in Full World", *Scientific American India*, Vol. 1, No. 4, September 2005, pp. 64–71. The author criticises reliance on the concept of the EKC. Ramawsamy Iyer in *Towards Water Wisdom* (2007) has doubts on this EKC argument. At the other end Pradipto Ghosh has praised the EKC and has shown its positive impact in India. See Prodipto Ghosh, "Harmonizing Environmental Concerns and Economic Growth", *Environment Matters*, The World Bank, 2004.
4. B.B. Vohra, *Natural Resources Management for Poverty Alleviation*, Rajiv Gandhi Institute for Contemporary Studies (RGICS), RGICS Paper

Number 35, 1996. The author was the Chairman of Advisory Group, Department of Wasteland Development.

5. Classical literature in this genre includes N.S. Jodha, "Common Property Resources and the Rural Poor" in Ramachandra Guha (ed.), *Social Ecology*, New Delhi: Oxford University Press, 1994, pp. 150-87; and Kanchan Chopra and S.C. Gulati, *Migration, Common Property Resources and Environmental Degradation*, New Delhi: Sage, 2001.
6. See Professor S.P. Banerjee, "A review of the environment management practices in the Indian mining sector" and Mrinal K. Ghose, "Soil conservation for rehabilitation and revegetation of mine-degraded land", in *TIDEE* (TERI Information Digest on Energy and Environment), 4(2) (June 2005): 127-36 and 137-50, respectively.
7. *Ecosystem and Human Well-Being: Synthesis, A Report of the Millennium Ecosystem Assessment, UN Millennium Ecosystem Assessment Report*, New York: World Resources Institute, 2005.
8. Barik *et al.*, "Jobs, Jobs, Jobs", *Down to Earth*, 30 November 2004: 26-34.
9. See, for example, Arun Shourie, *Governance and the Sclerosis that has set in* (New Delhi: Rupa, 2004), p. 196 and former minister and member of Parliament Brigadier K.P. Singh Deo, AVSM (Retd), Key Note Address during TA Seminar *Vision 2020* at New Delhi on 6 February 2006.
10. *India's Technology Needs: Nuclear to rural*, Second Darbari Seth Memorial Lecture, 26 August 2003, delivered by Dr R. Chidambaram, Principal Scientific Adviser to Government of India, New Delhi, TERI, 2003. The Presidential address was delivered by Shri George Fernandes. In November 2007, a study group of Himalayan glaciers has been instituted by the Principal Scientific Adviser to the Government of India, who is also chairing the recently constituted Expert Group on Impacts of Climate Change. The study group is responsible to gather all the relevant data related to Himalayan Glacier, its interpolation and to create a sharing mechanism with all the stakeholder organisations in the country. See <http://www.tifac/org.in/Himalayan/home.htm>.
11. Brigadier K.P. Singh Deo, AVSM (Retd), Key Note Address, n. 9.
12. *Report of the National Forest Commission*, Chairman Justice B.N. Kirpal, Government of India, Ministry of Environment and Forests, 2006, Chapter 8, "Forest Conservation", p. 108.
13. *Ibid.*, Chapter 9.16, "Involvement of the Military and Paramilitary", pp. 137-8.
14. *Ibid.*
15. P.K. Gautam, "Changing Geographical Factors in Planning and Conduct of Indian Military Operations", *Strategic Analysis*, March–April 2008, 32(2): 245-58.

16. Ashish Bose, "Malaria Deaths in Rajasthan Desert", *Economic and Political Weekly*, 19 June 2004: 2557–9; and Ashish Bose, "Stalling the March of Thar Desert", *Economic and Political Weekly*, 26 April 2003: 1630–2.
17. *The Hindu* (New Delhi), 10, 11 and 16 June 2007.
18. As the book was to go to press in early 2009, it has been learnt that under the Indo- German technical cooperation, The Delhi government has bid for CDM based on the restoration of Bhhati mines/afforestation being done by 132 Infantry Battalion (TA) Ecological which is fully funded by the Delhi government.
19. Some unethical practices in CDM projects were also exposed by the Centre for Science and Environment. See *Down to Earth*, 15 November 2005: 20–9. This was even referred to in the influential policy journal *Foreign Affairs*, which expressed serious doubts about the efficacy of the deals. It showed that Indian authorities seemed to have approved the project not on their merit but on the basis of the prestige of the consultant who validated them. See Ruth Greenspan Bell, "What to Do About Climate Change", *Foreign Affairs*, May/June 2006: 105–13.
20. This idea was presented during the TA Vision Seminar in February 2006. The Indian Army may also plan to take an active part in carbon trading (Clean Development Mechanism), not only through the way of ETF but in sustainable management of defence land in its charge. Another government agency which is very active in this field is the Indian Railways. In the post Kyoto arrangement beyond 2012, assisting in deforestation, rather than reforestation may also be included. In the present arrangement only some planting projects are allowed under Kyoto Protocol's CDM. The military is also deployed in operational areas on our borders and indirectly helps in the preservation of forests in addition to the defence land in its charge. Work for such a contingency can begin now to take a proactive part in the post-2012 funding mechanism. This survey will also provide a good consolidation of our forest cover under the military's influence. It will be a no- regret option.
21. *The Hindustan Times* (New Delhi), 24 November 2005.
22. I am thankful to Professor C.R. Babu for my visit to the Centre for Environmental Management of Degraded Ecosystem, School of Environmentàl Studies, University of Delhi in August and November 2005. I thank Dr Amit Love for his briefing and also a guided tour of the microbiology–bacteria laboratory. The CEMDE also has created the gene pool for plants for the afforestation done by the Delhi-based 132 ETF. The CEMDE studied the entire Aravali in a holistic and integrated manner to understand the problem of Bhatti mines. Dr Love also explained when not to remove Congress grass. This ecological wisdom needs to be converted into a manual for use by

the military and in all the important languages of India. He also corroborated what I learnt with the ETF—the ills of having non-native vilayati kikar all over the countryside. But I found that this knowledge was not in public domain. Later I was delighted to read in the newspapers about the good work done by CEMDE in creating thirty-four city forests, including Aravali Biodiversity Park in the capital and their battle to get rid of many invasive and intrusive species and revival of water bodies.

23. The old ways of doing things are constantly being swept away to make way for new ones. The term was coined by Joseph Schumpeter in *Capitalism, Socialism and Democracy* (1942). See *The Economist*, 24 November 2007.
24. Kemal Dervis, Administrator, UNDP and Achim Stiener, Executive director, UNEP, Foreword, *Human Development Report 2007/2008*, <http://hdr.undp.org/en/reports/global/hdr2007-2008/>, accessed on 29 November 2007.
25. My comments: While serving in 28 Infantry Division in 1988-89 I recall how the unprecedented rainfall during summer badly damaged the murals at the Basgo monastery-cum-fort near Nimu (near Leh). The General Officer Commanding the then Major General V.R. Raghavan rushed immediate engineer support to undo the damage.

8

Environmental Agenda for the Military and for Military-to-Military Cooperation

Preservation and protection of the marine environment, prevention and control of marine pollution, enforcement of maritime laws and collection of scientific data at sea are the "environmental" charter of the duties of the Indian Coast Guard. As has been shown in Chapter 2, the Indian Army is the only army in the world to have Ecological Task Forces (ETF) in action. The military in its peace locations, operational areas and naval/air bases has made ecological restoration and greening a normal practice. With UNEP's assistance under the Montreal Protocol the Defence Research and Development Organisation (DRDO) has set up a halon bank with active participation of the Indian Air Force and the other services.[1] The Indian Army and Green Governance is a theme on the web site of the Bombay Natural History Society. The army is the largest landholder in the country (8.5 million hectares), with establishments located in different ecosystems and bio-geographic zones, with 62 cantonments, 192 military stations, depots/training establishments, manoeuvre areas, firing ranges and military farms. More number of ETFs are being raised on the request of the state governments and the role of the military as a stakeholder is getting recognised.[2]

Environmental Agenda for the Military

Disaster Management

The lessons of the tsunami, extreme rainfall events of 2005 and the earthquake in Jammu and Kashmir of October 2005 have generated professional and focused needs which need to be addressed by the military. India has a high population density. Minimum mitigation against disasters like earthquake-tolerant buildings has not been done. Flood plains have been reclaimed for urban growth. Construction of infrastructure like roads and embankment for railway tracks has congested drainage of natural river channels, upsetting the natural flow and intensifying extreme flood events. Combined with the early symptoms of climate change like increased frequency of floods and droughts, disasters relate directly to the subject of environmental security. The future adverse effects of climate change will be massive disaster events. A National Disaster Management Authority (NDMA) has been set up. Dealing with disasters is now in the ambit of the Ministry of Home Affairs. The recently constituted Administrative Reforms Commission is studying the issue further. The role of the armed forces in disaster management is likely to decrease further. However, because of the capability and flexibility of the military and its location in or near disaster-prone areas, it is unlikely that the demands for "aid to civil authority" by the state governments will decline. Tasks as first respondents would need to be performed by the military. The military may be the only effective instrument of state power in dealing with international and cross-border disasters. Ecological intelligence suggests that these disasters may increase in intensity and frequency.

Military Training and the Environment

Before the Green Revolution the standard practice in northern India was to train on manoeuvre in peak summer after the harvest of rabi crop. With muti-cropping and multiple pressures on land this now is unthinkable. Rajasthan continues to be the preferred location for manoeuvres and firing, including nuclear tests. The number of field firing ranges (acquired and notified) in the country have reduced due to pressures of urbanisation, population growth and land scarcity. As conventional wars have receded, the idea of "training for war" is also changing. One school is that we need to do away with large scale manoeuvres and live firing. The other school argues not to do the grave error of cutting down live training. As long as war as a social phenomenon exists, militaries would need to be trained with realism. The debate on the cost benefit analysis of the need of training areas versus the human and ecological factors is unlikely to end soon.[3] Political pressures is generated to denotify ranges in some instances. Use of simulators is one arguments put forth by theoreticians to do away with field firing ranges. Ironically the field firing range and the environs are having the best conservation. This can be seen at Devlali and Ahmadnagar. What needs to be realised is that the impact area is just a very small percentage of the range where the shell bursts. Barring that, the other areas are having luscious trees. In the 1980s Bombay Natural History Society (BNHS) had studied bird hazard and flight safety for the Indian Air Force. The process is being repeated to cater for the change in human and bird population and characteristics. Mismanaged urban garbage attracting birds rather than only trees per se are a greater threat to flight safety. One classic case of closing the fighter base at Hindon in the 1980s was due to un-disposed carcasses of the meat industry attracting kites and similar birds. This happened due to population pressures and urbanisation. More fighter bases are under the assault of concrete jungles cum waste to close down.

Human Security

A new human security angle is emerging in the displaced persons from the ranges. In Jharkhand there is an agitation resisting the acquiring of Netarhat ranges for the defence services. These areas are also Naxal affected. But in nearly all the ranges in the country, one narrative which may need to be studied is the political economy of 'sikka (metals and splinters) pickers' who descend like ants on spilled sugar the moment firing practices terminate. Linked to poverty, it is much more hazardous than the ship-breaking industry (as the harvest also includes unexploded shells or blinds/duds). This informal and illegal industry supplies the Indian economy cheap iron and brass. Contractor mafia has also emerged. Human and ecological implications of the training and testing needs can not be wished away. More nuanced and sensitive understanding of 'national security' as a result of ecological and human factors would be desired.

Military Installations

At the suggestion of the Commandant College of Defence Management, one work has already appeared in *Current Science* on environmental management of defence installations for sustainability.[4] Officers on study leave in prestigious institutions such as the Indian Institute of Technology (IIT) are studying military-environmental interface as it pertains to installations and ranges.[5]

Military-to-Military Cooperation

Military-to-military cooperation on environmental matters may emerge as an important tool of diplomacy in the region. A common ecological system such as the Himalayas is shared by most of the militaries of the region. In 2001 a joint US-India seminar was held on Himalayan ecology. This was followed by a series of joint service Indo-US tabletop exercises at the USI of India on maritime pollution in the Indian Ocean. Some areas in military-to-military cooperation are as under:

China

In international negotiations like the issue of climate change India needs to coordinate the negotiation position with China as the two countries have similar interests. Common concerns with China are on issues such as emissions, adverse impact of climate change, and energy. There is also a need to have a transparent mechanism on India's concerns with the flow of rivers. China has since joined the convention on the prohibition of military or any other hostile use of environmental modification technique (ENMOD). To have greater transparency and trust, there is a need to have data sharing and joint study of the water flow including glacier retreat and meltdown of Tibetan permafrost which may affect the railway track. The Sutlej and the Brahmaputra originate in Tibet. For meaningful confidence-building measures India's concerns with flash floods due to natural causes such as landslides upstream in Tibet may require greater military-to-military cooperation to build trust.

Pakistan

The glaciers and other similar ecosystems will demand the study of the ecological degradation and disposal of waste in the glacial region of the river systems. Pollution control measures may require joint monitoring of the waste and its safe disposal. Military-to-military cooperation is one way to get the fastest and practical results. Besides glaciers, there is a need to restore the forests and ecology of the entire militarised zones in Jammu and Kashmir. Population growth has placed heavy demands on the fixed water assets. Rather than just trading charges over sharing of the water in accordance with the Indus Water Treaty (IWT), joint watershed restoration may bring better supply of water in the long term. Restoration of the lakes by an ETF would result in better flow on the Jhelum. A stage may soon be reached when reforestation and afforestation can be done beyond both sides of the Line of Control (LoC) once infiltration ceases. Restoring the vegetation and revival of the watershed would lead to a better climate for economic development. In the Indus basin in the plains both India and Pakistan face waterlogging and salinity. The Pakistan Army desilts the canals in Punjab. Salinity and waterlogging are common problems. The Indira Gandhi Nehar Prayojna (IGNP) command area in Rajasthan slopes north-east to south-west towards Sind. This gives rise to problems of drainage. India is enjoined by the IWT not to permit pollution of stream flow into Pakistan. This precludes flow of polluted water draining into Sutlej as it leaves India. As recommended by the National Commission for Integrated Water Resources Development satisfactory disposal of saline water from IGNP command area may lie in negotiating with Pakistan, for an outlet to its left bank outfall drain or other system in Sind on the basis of quid pro quo. Though not part of the IWT, the seepage from IGNP has helped groundwater recharge and greening in areas along the border region of Pakistan. As these canals and drains (like all rivers and canals on either side) are also military obstacles, greater military-to-military cooperation may dispel the historical baggage of mistrust and revive both the surface and groundwater regime of the Indus basin. One stumbling-block on the IWT treaty and run-of-the-river projects is the perception in Pakistan that India can use the dams to flood and deny approaches. Simulation studies show that the flooding issue is overblown. Another phobia is control of water by India to cause desertification in Pakistan. Both phobias need to be dispelled.

Former Foreign Secretary Jagat Mehta recounts how he made his team work overnight to see the imaginary "national security" implications of India tinkering with the water of Chenab at Salal either to cause flood or desertification.

> Although Salal had been discussed a score of times, we from India had never seriously attempted to expose them as technically fallacious and even contingency-wise unsound.... I urged one or two of our irrigation and power engineers led by R. Rangachari and Leela Poonappa who were part of our negotiating team, to examine a worst-case contingency as if they were Pakistanis. I requested them to draw up a balance sheet of possible loss and damage if, in fact, we were to abuse the storage at Salal in the way probably suspected by the Pakistani diplomatic professional and technical experts.... Our officers concluded that the impact of a peremptory release of the stored waters from a dam site 30 miles inside the frontiers would substantially be contained within Indian controlled Jammu and Kashmir itself. The storage capacity being limited, the residuary flow would have greatly reduced the hypothetical flood damage in the adjoining areas of Pakistan. They also worked out that from such a one-shot release and temporary slowing down of the river flow, the reduction in the availability of water for the canals would, at best, delay the downstream irrigation cycle but one to one-half days. This would be insufficient to do permanent harm to standing wheat crop in which normal watering cycle is once in three weeks.[6]

Simulation software and models now can easily be run jointly for a better scientific understanding. The imagined and exaggerated "security implication" of Baglihar which is further upstream can also be similarly dispelled. But this would require sustained hard work and regular interactions between the water bureaucracy and the military of both countries. Lessons and good practices from exchanging the data on nuclear installations as on 1 January each year must now be transferred to water sharing issues which go beyond the fine print of the Indus Water Treaty.

Bangladesh

Inland waterways would be a good communication links to the North-East. In the past, Bangladesh objected to the Indian proposal for a link to Farakka through Bangladesh. The Indian proposal to link the Brahmaputra via Bangladesh to overcome the problem of Farakka barrage was also objected to by China, as in the past it was considered a means of military communications. In the light of better relations with China there is a need to re-engage on this issue with Bangladesh. This has also to be approached in the light of the fear of Bangladesh about the proposed linking of rivers in India. Much of the historical mistrust can be overcome by better cooperation, including military-to-military cooperation. Revitalisation of the Sunderbans mangroves is another area for cooperation by a joint ETF. Another feature that needs further analysis is the sediment load being discharged in the Ganga, Brahmaputra and Meghna delta region leading to sediment shift or appearing of new land features in the coastal areas on which rival claims are made. Rapprochement will also generate scientific understanding of the phenomenon of floods. India will have to do a great deal of hard work to dispel the myth that all flood events in Bangladesh are India's doing. New research on watershed management needs to be pursued. *Forest and Flood: Drowning in fiction or thriving on facts?*, an FAO/CIFOR study, has shown that

> A common reaction is to blame the mismanagement of Asia's uplands and the clearing of forests in important mountainous watersheds for misery brought to the lowlands. To a large extent, conventional wisdom—which is sometimes more fiction than fact—about the benefits of forests has clouded the perspective of

> decision-makers, leading to an over-emphasis on reforestation and forest protection at the expense of more holistic watershed and river-basin management.[7]

Perhaps the most important environment-security link with Bangladesh is the forthcoming sea-level rise due to global warming and delta subsidence. Low-lying coastal regions of Bangladesh are vulnerable. These ecological refugees would add further tensions to the illegal migrants issue between India and Bangladesh.

Nepal

The maximum catchment of the Ganga basin is in Nepal. As has been shown in Chapter 4, restoration of forest cover could be one area of assistance to the Nepal Army to organise the people on ETF basis. This would also permit people's willing participation and may in addition help in countering insurgencies as it will generate employment.

Maritime Neighbours

The maritime neighbours need to be engaged in pollution response measures. All coastlines are vulnerable to oil spills. With the growth of the world economy and consequent growth in the traffic of oil tankers the danger of oil spills is increasing. Greater military-to-military cooperation and planning for contingencies would make our maritime neighbours more responsive. The Indian Coast Guard's present capacity is to handle 10,000 tons of oil spill. A grey area is that once the oil spill hits the shore, the labour-intensive cleaning up is that of an organisation on land. There is a limit to mobilising volunteers for such sustained work. Joint strategies need to be worked out for dealing with oil spill spreading to neighbouring countries' coastal regions.

Indian waters are also convenient burial sites for derelict bottoms. Taking advantage of lax insurance and monitoring mechanism, it becomes easy for the crew of ships flying flags of convenience to abandon the vessel with polluting or hazardous cargo. The coast guard and the navies of the region need to gear up to prevent the Indian Ocean from being treated as a dump-site. As single-hulled ships get phased out in developed countries, they are likely to head to Indian waters.

NOTES

1. Halon, a fire-fighting chemical, is being phased out on account of its ozone damaging potential. India being a developing country is allowed its centralised use till 2010 after which it would be phased out. Replacement research and national halon banking is the responsibility of the Centre for Fire Explosives and Environmental Safety (CFEES) under the DRDO. The IAF is the largest user of halon. The Indian Army, Indian Navy, and the Indian Coast Guard also use it substantially. Thanks to Dr K.C. Wadhwa of CFEES for showing me the laboratory and providing literature and to Wing Commander Prem of Air Headquartes for explaining its use in the IAF. Telephonically officers of the Army, Naval and Coast Guard Headquarters were most helpful in providing information. With effect from 2009, Headquarter Technical Group, Electronic and Mechanical Engineers have been nominated as a nodal agency for ozone related matters.
2. *Green Governance*, at <http://www.fao.org/documents/show_cdr.asp?url_file=docrep/v7850e/v7850e12htm>, accessed in August 2005. I am thankful to Colonel Prakash Tewari, Director, Policy (Ecology) QMG Branch, Army Headquarters for providing me with information including on the future role of the military.
3. According to media reports, the number of field firing ranges have shrunk over the last two and a half decades—from 104 ranges to seven by 2014. Currently the army has 40 notified ranges. See *Hindustan Times* (New Delhi), December, 12, 2008.
4. N.H. Rao, "Environmental Management: Relevance and implications for management of defence installations for sustainability", *Current Science*, 88(11) (10 June 2005): 1753-8.
5. Internet correspondence of author with Lieut Col K.N. Narasimha of IIT, Kanpur in 2005.
6. Jagat Mehta, *Negotiating for India: Resolving problems through diplomacy (Seven case studies 1958-1978)*, New Delhi: Manohar, 2006, pp. 207-8.
7. He Changchui, Assistant Director-General and Regional Representative for Asia and the Pacific FAO, Foreword, *Forest and Flood: Drowning in fiction or thriving on facts?*, The United Nations, Food and Agriculture Organization (FAO) and The Center for International Forestry Research (CIFOR), RAP Publication 2005/03, Forest Perspective, 2005, p. v.

9

Conclusions

Environmental security is an important and emerging agenda in security studies and has now been included as an issue in international relations. Placing it in security perspective, we need to ask the three classical questions of security: security for whom? security from what? and who provides security?

As the work of the ETFs and the culture of ecological preservation by the military in various types of terrain shows, a battle is being waged to preserve our ecology. To answer the question security for whom, we can say that security is being provided to help us grow and develop in a sustainable way. Here both the state and the individual are involved. Or we can say that both state and human security is being implied. The question security from what is more complex. We need to protect our land, watersheds and forests from environmental degradation—which is more due to human actions than natural events. Environmental degradation is likely to aggravate due to adverse impacts of climate change. Our natural capital needs to be saved. The third question of who provides security is the core issue or the thesis statement of this work. It goes beyond the increasing role of the military in disasters. Here the military has a new role, though not mandated, but similar to the term "mission creep". The military mind and ethos, due to its training in defence and security is professionally inclined to assess all types of threats. At the same time, due to inertia of realist thinking, the standing military remains deployed and ready for combat all the time. The last interstate war between India and Pakistan was fought in 1971 and a limited one in 1999. Counterinsurgency operations is another secondary job which the military has been performing. The next mission, which is emerging, is military and environmental interface. Within the country, there is sufficient evidence to show adverse or chronic environmental degradation. Those who deny environmental degradation are no better than those who perceive India only in terms of GDP and stock market. Our path of economic development, as we have seen, would continue to degrade the environment. We cannot ignore the end state—which is deforestation, desertification, loss of arable land due to salinisation, waterlogging and soil nutrient exhaustion, renewable resource scarcities like that of land and water, and tragic loss of biodiversity resulting in loss of resilience. We still have not reached a hopeless end state of beyond recovery. But if nothing is done and we continue business as usual, the collapse of the ecosystem and resources scarcities is likely to happen soon. Crucial ecosystems such as the Himalayas are threatened. We also need to take measures to mitigate climate change by way of afforestation, cutting down excess greenhouse gas emissions and other activities of land use. Adaptation to adverse impacts of climate change is of equal importance. Through ecological restoration, we attempt both mitigation and adaptation.

Addressing the environment-human interface also makes us aware of the phenomenal diversity of our country, not only in people, religion, ethnicity, language and so on, but in terms of biodiversity and relationship with Nature. The military is a reflection of society; now there is a reverse feedback in progress. The military as it tends to Nature is an early warning ecological sensor. Larger ecological issues like relationship of people with land in Rajasthan or the abandoned terraced fields in Kumaon or the debates over jhum show how ecological issues must be studied in a larger national security framework, a framework that goes beyond just the threat of an invasion by a foreign military.

The military by way of ETF of the Territorial Army has demonstrated just one way how ecological restoration can be done. Expanding the role requires political will. In the present stage of traditional security challenges, it will be most unwise to change the primary mission of the military from territorial integrity to environmental preservation. What can be done is to understand the military-like ethos and discipline to fight this battle, rather than to militarise the environment. In civil-military relations, environmental protection at a national scale is not possible by the military alone. However, best practices can be extracted for other sectors of civil society.

Another conclusion may be that the military may be tasked to take care of environmental degradation of remote and harsh regions as in our border areas. Here, as ecological fragility does not respect sovereign boundaries, there is a new and renewed case for a greater role of military-to-military cooperation by the militaries of neighbours. The coast guard has been involved in joint ventures, but the military deployed on the borders also now needs to study this emerging challenge and solve it through military cooperation. The hinterland could be organised on models such as the ETF, similar to the institutionalisation of the NCC.

Simultaneously, as India urbanises and so do the soldiers, the military must take measures to preserve its ecological performance and base of knowledge to undertake this task directly linked to Nature. Centres of excellence must emerge with scientific documentation and literature as to how to go about ecological work in military garrisons and field stations.

Non-traditional security threats such as the environment cannot be tackled by the traditional instruments of security apparatus like the military alone. As the chapters on field visits to some selected parts of India showed, there are emerging challenges, which are beyond the military, that need to be addressed. Policy issues like Inner Line restrictions of biodiversity storehouse in Arunachal Pradesh, a greater understanding of pastoralists as the military combats desertification by greening the desert, multidisciplinary issues of how to build and maintain roads better in the young Himalayas, how to get rid of intrusive species and monoculture forestry for better watershed management also emerge from this study. We also need to be more sensitive to the social and cultural customs and traditions that the diverse people of India follow. Much is linked to traditional ecological knowledge, which at times we wrongly presume is primitive and thus unscientific. The military posted at the border regions can consolidate this knowledge for future use.

To reiterate, although this study began with the role of the military and environment, it could not ignore the larger ecological challenges that we face. Many challenges have security implications in the new understanding of the term. If some ideas and suggestions are incorporated in policy circles we could say that we may be doing the right thing for environmental security. The study has also shown some new areas for further studies, and some gaps too. This may also help the academic community in further consolidation of knowledge peculiar to our country. Lastly, this may be a work which may inspire the general public to relate to this new security challenge and help in generating a new consciousness in the nation.

Index